EX CATHEDRAS

(IX - XV)

Copyright © 2013 by Peter Joannides
All rights reserved.

This book or any portion thereof may not be reproduced or used in any manner whatsoever without the express written permission of the publisher except for the use of brief quotations in a book review.

Printed in the United States of America

Corrected second printing, 2019

ISBN 978-0-9892536-4-2

www.PetroulisI@gmail.com

PREFACE

The **Ex Cathedras** in this volume are part of a longer series begun in 1972 and continued to the present day (spanning over 41 years and totaling 23 installments). The first eight are embedded in my major work *Amán Amán!* (Amazon, 2013)—the initial three published in the Jacksonville University newspaper "The Navigator" and simply photographed with all mistakes and warts remaining as they were. (**Ex Cathedras 4** through **8**, however, were edited.)

When I completed *Amán Amán!* I never again wanted to involve myself in anything so painful as the sort of writing I had been doing. Every writing bout was like being led to an inquisition chamber. I knew I had created something of value, but I didn't want to go through any more agony. In addition, I felt I had accomplished what I set out to accomplish.

However, I did want to keep my hand in. My love of language, literature, and writing had not abated. And so I continued with the **Ex Cathedras**, writing one at a time with sometimes as many as four years separating one from the next, but usually about a year or two.

Writing the **Ex Cathedras** was not painful—just the reverse. I would simply wait until the thought occurred, and then record it. After which I would embellish, improve, adjust, try to perfect. Unlike the efforts with the Magnum Opus, this process was pleasurable and delightful.

Nearly all the **Ex Cathedras** were privately printed in the form of a small spiral-bound booklet, in which a page had to be turned for each entry. To duplicate this original form would no doubt be commercially prohibitive, and so in this volume, roughly four entries are included on each page.

It has become obvious to me in reviewing these past **Ex Cathedras** that there are many duplications and hardly disguised repetitions. I suppose I may owe the Reader an apology. However, it should be borne in mind that years would elapse from one **Ex Cathedra** to the next, I would forget, and certain themes were clearly and repeatedly occupying my mind more than others. Certainly these repetitions could have been editorially excised from the present book, but I wanted to be faithful to the originals and, more importantly, to the time and spirit of the moments I lived. Perhaps the best justification and defense is that each **Ex Cathedra** should be looked upon as an autonomous unit, and judged accordingly.

Some entries were minimally edited relative to the booklet originals.

Peter Joannides

CONTENTS

Ex Cathedra 9	1
Ex Cathedra 10	49
Ex Cathedra 11	97
Ex Cathedra 12	149
Ex Cathedra 13	197
Ex Cathedra 14	259
Ex Cathedra 15	321

May 20, 1991

Ex Cathedra

9th Encyclical

von Herrn Doktor Professor Peter Joannides

I

Maybe I should be the **deus ex machina** for **somebody else.**

II

One can hang on to the consciousness of a mood for only so long.

III

What have I to say to anyone who likes motorcycles?

IV

In all the varieties of human link and nexus and the untold plethora,

Only a parent to a child is not a stranger.

V

Sex is essentially proprietary, predatory, anti-social.

It cannot and should not be brought into the open.

VI

Unbeknownst to us, we create and live the (soon-to-be) most nostalgic of traditions—all along the way.

VII

I want to ram my particularity right down everyone's throat.

VIII

Life's too frangible and short not to tell the truth.

IX

I can drink cranberry juice cocktail, every day, all day long.

(Here ends the excerpt from the uncompleted **Ex Cathedra 9** included in the major work *Amán Amán!*)

Ninth Encyclical

1

How I wish I, like Edmond Dantès, could return from the dead to reward my friends and haunt my enemies.

2

For a philosopher, one stamp of suffering can stand the stead of all sorts of suffering.

3

How I love books published between 1888 and 1910, with lithographs, engravings, and whilom sketches preceded and protected by gauzy and onion-thin velutinous pages.

4

I have burned so many bridges, I no longer even **think** about not getting wet.

5

There is such a thing as a literary-philosophical awareness, that is both rarer and higher than either a literary one or a philosophical one.

6

Committing suicide for not winning the Lotto,

Is one of the most legitimate reasons for doing so.

7

The hubbub and conviviality of mealtime amongst family and friends.

All else to pale before such glees and godsends.

8

It is very lonely not to be a cog.

9

There is something about India that draws and redraws and redraws.

10

There was a time when there was no time.

Nor death, nor deception, nor decay, nor torpor, nor disillusion.

11

We are helpless in a dream.

Not so, when we awake.

12

There is a sense in which Whitman is painfully transparent.

And also, not a particularly good poet.

13

It has always appalled me: why anyone would want to accomplish **little** things.

14

I have probably lived a most excellent life, without even realizing it.

15

George F. Kennan sounds like a good man.

16

At exactly 5 $^{27}/_{60}$ minutes out from the freezer, when it just **begins** to turn into a soupy slushy mush, ice cream is at its best.

17

I can't tell you how much I have enjoyed reading Edmondo de Amicis' **Constantinople** (published 1896).

A heart after my own soul.

18

The slightest most minuscule pressure on my bladder doth mightily disturb me.

19

I resent being patronized by groupie ill-mannered middling two-bit editors and literary agents.

20

As little vindictive as I am in my personal doings, so much and all the more so in my writing.

21

If I **did** believe in reincarnation, and if I **had** to choose some shadowy and elusive former life, it would have something to do with the heyday of British India.

And then there were Biarritz and Deauville.

22

Most people are not worth a minim damn.

23

I don't mind digging ditches, but I **do** mind talking to people who dig ditches.

24

I can rightfully skim through another's work; no one can rightfully skim through mine.

25

There are B.F. (before-fame) friends and A.F. (after-fame) friends, and the only ones you can truly trust are the former.

26

Bad poets are sometimes good people.

And the converse.

27

I only **seem** erudite and well-read because I invariably allude to the few writers I do know something about.

Think of the far vaster reach and backdrop of those I don't know anything about.

28

All these encyclopaedic pretenses and prances—these cockalorum intellectual swaggers—do thoroughly distaste me.

29

Henry Miller is **family**; perhaps even more so than Thomas Wolfe.

30

I want to have a **personal** relationship with: my barber, my doctor, my lawyer, my tailor, my druggist, my mechanic, my travel-agent, my waiter, my banker, my postman, my publisher.

31

You either live under a star, or you don't.

32

Some people think locally; others nationally; yet others internationally.

33

Presidents, kings, directors, generals, governors, executives, commanders cannot really enjoy themselves.

Too much on their mind.

34

I have no skeletons in **my** closet. They're all hanging and jiggling upon the rafters.

35

All these vortices and perspectives, one after another, continuously conspire to suck me in.

But in the end, I refuse to be sucked in.

36

Sometimes I **like** to use a magnitudinous word where a short one will do.

37

The work of Ben Belitt and Lawrence Durrell is so **dense**, it just densily disappears.

38

However lofty and grand the cosmic perspective, it must take into account the case of the quadriplegic who begged to be let die.

39

Some things that can be spoken, cannot be written.

And vice versa.

40

    I still live in a courtly world where letters are answered, telephone calls returned, pledges honored, and talk of money matters a bit discomfiting.

41

Kissing is more intimate than fucking.

42

Henry Miller is not in the least vulgar.

Allen Ginsberg is.

43

    I have pretty much decided: the anguish and ecstasy of writing, the very highest calling.

44

Many writers' (including the best of them) **theories** of what they do are sometimes quite laughable.

45

I am probably much more **specialized** than I think I am.

46

I don't know why I consider taking part in commercials so reprehensible, but there it is.

Reprehensible.

In fact, downright sickening and immoral.

47

Please: Spare me henceforth from Jewish intellectuals all entangled-coiled in the throes of their Jewishness.

48

Four eager, amiable, personable, decent young Australians telling us about the wonders of the 21st Century.

And then, out of the blue, the sudden cold-shower injection of the brash, vulgar, phony, plastic American voice of Sharon Nash.

49

Over the years, I have been mainly **confused** by Australians.

But as time goes by, I more and more warm up to them.

50

The object of writing is to stop writing.

51

Writers (even the best of them) are adolescents.

52

What can be more absurd than the English fox hunt?

53

When something grabs me, it just grabs me.

I no longer wish to **work** at something grabbing me.

54

Memo to MacLeish: A poet may take an interest in human affairs, perhaps even passionately so, but he cannot work for the government.

55

It is tragic to have gone through life without a visit to Torres del Paine.

56

I could no more write fiction than the man in the moon.

57

Once one has had a glimpse of The Aleph, how can one bear settling for anything less?

58

I give no quarter; I ask for no quarter.

59

Journalists are smart, but they are not the smartest.

60

There are children.

Then there are grown-up second-order children.

And then even aged third-order children.

61

I like people who like Wolfe.

62

I don't mind working as long as I don't have to teach, sell, or serve.

63

Ah to rummage round the ruins of Taormina, under the nuzzly sunlight.

64

While the birds chirrupy chirp and children rompingly play and cricketers and picnickers and promenaders shuffle saunter on fields of clover and their lazy sway,

    there are those on dialysis machines.

65

    What is in and of itself inane,

    Is, to a child, rapt and wondrous.

66

What is so disgusting is not so much that teaching has to be done, but that some teachers actually, thirstily, **enjoy** what they do.

67

Leo Buscaglia is essentially a rabble-rouser, but he rouses the rabble in the right direction.

68

I used to think that every single Cypriot was a member of this warm and good and kindly and magnanimous lot.

But now I know there are some bad eggs in the basket.

69

When all is said and done, and after all the misgivings, musings, second thoughts, soul searchings, ambivalences…

I simply must have my quota of rich red meat.

70

As long as there are wildflowers,

I've got to hang in there.

71

But for a woman's wanton wiles, Suleiman the Magnificent would not have murdered his best friend as well as his first-born son.

72

Oh how they strut, all those popinjays and cock-a-hoops,

In **The New York Times Book Review** and **The New York Review of Books**.

73

As time goes by, times get so thoroughly jumbled—and chronology begins to wear a face more and more incidental.

74

I like to garner history,
obliquely.

75

The one advantage I have over many a predecessor,

Is that most all my references, asides, allusions,

Are most indelibly filed on film and tape and script and record.

76

The idea that Helen Keller really did earn a college degree is really a bit ridiculous.

77

Countries are not people.

78

Melina Mercouri makes for an excellent Greek; but a floundering and somewhat embarrassing **femme international**.

79

Ofelia Schutte writing about Nietzsche.

Here we have arrogance compounded by impertinent and sacrilegious presumption.

Hardly anything more knotted, disgusting, and ugly can be imagined.

80

Politeness doesn't ring true in an American.

81

It has now become clear, what was only vaguely before apprehended:

Max Black was a dilettante.

82

I used to hate Bette Davis as a kid.

Now there is heartfelt admiration.

83

One can be provincial in time,

Just as easily as in space.

84

What more astonishing and appalling? What people will do for money.

85

What more rueful, disconcerting, depressing, amazing? **How people spend their time.**

86

All the intelligence, sophistication, sensitivity, vitality don't amount to a hill o' beans without an element of courage.

87

Buchwald is no Benchley.

88

The most stunningly, breathtakingly, exquisitely beautiful woman—with a New York accent.

Forget it.

89

Lawrence really didn't know the first thing about sex.

90

It's a shame that Arab women, who can otherwise be so ripplingly velvety beautiful, have to have such horse-faces.

91

The trouble with Richard Burton is that he was always **declaiming.**

92

The best thing about Vincent Price is his love of food.

93

There is something about a tracheotomy that thoroughly depresses and undoes me.

94

So many whores, of one sort or another, male and female, old and young, everywhere and all about, throughout.

95

To have an income of anything less than an unencumbered, unfettered $300,000 per annum is to be in prison.

96

The BIG FOUR: Walter Bass, Eli Bassett, Charles Moore, Wayne Hamm.

97

The voice of Phillip Hinton is almost as good as that of Anthony Quayle.

98

Gore Vidal: Cecil B. DeMille Writ Large.

99

I am beginning to think the voice of Phillip Hinton is, in some ways, even better than that of Anthony Quayle.

100

Experience of the abstract is just that, and nothing more.

101

The ugliest sound on earth: that of a chain saw.

102

I simply cannot understand how anyone could have been so wise as Nietzsche.

103

No one in the Universe knows how to enjoy himself more than I.

104

No one is more interested in I than me.

105

A gilded prison is still a prison.

106

"Power corrupts and absolute power corrupts absolutely."

With respect to any decent and conscientious man, this is plain nonsense.

107

I don't like Archbishop Iakovos.

108

Anyone who would stand at a busy intersection on a sweltering day in May, in a coat and tie, holding his own election sign, and smiling-waving at all the cars and passers-by—

Is nothing less than a fawning ass-kissing bootlicking buffoon.

109

Work is not honorable; it is horrible.

110

I am beginning to prefer being with intelligent people I don't particularly like, to people I like who aren't particularly intelligent.

111

There may be few, very few, truly **sterling** people.

But then, so what?…what does it matter?

There are those few.

112

All my life I've been doing it: lavishly proffering my pearls before swine.

113

There is something a little bit obscene about Hume Cronyn-Jessica Tandy.

114

Why anyone would want to be Mayor, Congressman, Senator, Governor, Foreign Minister, President, is utterly beyond me.

Now **DICTATOR**…now that's another matter.

115

We must treat the Dead as if they were the Living.

Otherwise, the road to a drowning madness.

116

A man who is well-fed is apt to be more spiritual than one who is hungry.

117

Time is so precious, pressing, fleeting—sometimes there isn't enough time to even talk about time.

118

Not only do I have to contend with ignorance, ineptitude, injustice, vulgarity, undependableness, gracelessness—but, on top of all that, even with insidious and shifty little viruses, wayward cells, and all manner of germs as well.

119

Have you noticed that some computerees begin to resemble the taskmasters that they serve?

120

One's life could end (and could have ended) at **any** moment.

I wonder if anyone has ever thoroughly explored the implications of this?

121

Instead of worrying over fonts, typescripts, circumflexes, transliterations, point sizes, spaces, margins, what have you...

I should be chasing after phantoms.

122

Prolonged heavy rain is metaphysical.

123

Quality time.

As in the sentence, "I spent some quality time with my kids."

One of those distasteful, canty, groupie expressions all the more insidious for its smug and self-congratulating cut-above hauteur.

124

The world is full of amateurs.

125

The only way I would ever solve Rubic's Cube is by sheer and unadulterated **accident**.

126

What Rubic did, I could never in a million years do.

But I suspect that what I do, Rubic too could never in a million years do.

127

A Great Poet cannot also be a diplomat.

128

I can't believe my eyes and ears: all these glowing eulogies, tributes, and testimonials for dear-departed and hell-bound Norman Malcolm.

129

I could forgive a murderer before I could forgive Norman Malcolm.

130

It seems to me that the objective of mankind should be to create a whole race of Peter Joannideses.

131

Playing the Lotto may be foolhardy, but not so to the winner.

132

It's probably not a good idea to cross Peter Joannides.

133

I really don't know what it's like to be someone else, because I've always been me.

134

There really is no Long-Ago or Far-Away.

135

The more meticulous the mechanics, the more the message gets through.

136

Maya is the closest thing to that which could disabuse me of solipsism.

137

I can't stand professors. Just the look and whiff of them makes me nauseous.

138

If you must be a collector, why not collect beautiful women?

Or, better still, culinary marvels?

139

I love language.

140

I have done more or less what Proust has done—**and without the benefit of being sick!**

(At least not **obviously** so.)

141

My work is like Life itself: untidy, scraggly, capricious and moody and wobbly, full of contrarieties and oppositions, with hardly a grandiose conclusion or symphonic finale.

142

Sometimes an experience pales before the **description** of that experience.

143

I know of no one better suited to run this Planet than a dyed-in-the-wool hedonist.

144

Women who wear a ring on every finger are not women for me.

145

The highest good is Goodness.

146

I can't bear Greek dances danced by Greek-Americans.

147

I usually don't like people whom everybody likes, but even I like Father Paul Costopoulos.

148

Only a writer is not truly lonely.

149

Even more nettlesome than translations, are transliterations.

150

Children, other than one's own, are irritating.

151

There's something I like about important people who don't have unlisted numbers.

152

I can't believe I spent 41 years of my life pounding that rock, when all along there was another way.

153

I like or dislike people not any the more nor any the less, just because they've died.

154

Literature (Art, Music, History, a Documentary) is supposedly **about** something.

Actually it is about itself.

155

I covet other men's wives all the time.

156

It's not the distance, it's the lights that get you.

157

The local affairs and politics and social whirls of Jacksonville absolutely thrill me!

158

Poetry with an **obvious** and recurrent periodic rhyme is both fatuous and preposterous.

159

Sapelo Island has character.

160

AIDS is the most despicable of diseases.

161

Experience comes in bits and pieces, to be pieced together, later.

162

Times there are when thieving is more honorable than working.

163

I've hated Jacksonville for so long, I'm beginning to like it.

January 6, 1994

Ex Cathedra

10th Encyclical

von Herrn Doktor Professor Peter Joannides

1

I love to drive around a city,

In the dead of night.

2

I love company,

But I'll take my own lonesome company over most company.

3

When all is said and done, and compared assessed adjudged apprized,

I'll go with rum.

4

It's still fun to build sand castles, even though they'll soon be washed away.

5

...on the other hand, money can also falsify and isolate.

6

There really is Progress.

Razor blades used to always nick and scrape me. Now, with Gillette Atras, there is nothing of the sort.

7

Most of my friends are really peasants.

8

A thief is better than a salesman.

9

People die; things change; nothing is ever quite the same.

10

All principles are suspect, including this one.

11

Most people go to war, work at deathly boring jobs, follow prescribed rules and hackneyed patterns, give the proper responses, toe the lines of their pitiful lives in endless and meaningless repetitions: a world of corralled and shuffling baa-baaing sheep.

12

I know You Can't Go Home Again, but I would so much like to.

13

    I drive better with a couple of drinks; I don't see why pilots couldn't fly better with a couple of drinks.

14

    In spite of all the demurrals and denials, the truth is, there is hardly a soul that doesn't at sometime or other think about the lottery.

15

    Everything should be free; after all, everything was free to start with.

16

    Everyone is a cog, except the Walt Whitmans.

17

Walt Whitmans are the flower, the nectar, the very sense and purport, the absolution, the **raison d'être** of society.

18

What I like best about Whitman is the scope.

19

The most significant thing that happened to all those who have known Peter Joannides is that they have known Peter Joannides.

20

People really do **radically** change.

(I never really did think it was true.)

21

Tendons and ligaments heal so gradually,

So goddamned maddeningly grittingly screamingly gradually.

22

If it should turn out that Norman Cousins and I were not all that far different, I shall want to kill myself.

23

Norman Cousins: the second-rateness of the man shines brightly forth.

24

A suggestion to my Greek translator: I would leave the Romanized Greek phrases exactly as they are, thus indicating to the Greek reader that they are not translations from the English.

As for the few words and phrases written in the Greek alphabet itself, I leave that little problem up to you.

25

The only Southern voice I ever liked was that of Joseph Cotten.

26

Pain and Pleasure are absolutes. They cannot be argued for, against, about, with, over, or away.

27

I have been anti-American for a long long time.

Not in any political sense. Nor in any moral sense, or philosophical sense, or doctrinaire sense.

Just in an aesthetic sense.

28

Jazz simply just doesn't move me.

29

Although it sickens me to say it, I am probably, at heart, a Platonist.

30

There is no Time.

All Times are Simultaneous.

31

Handball and swimming—that's it. Any other exercise makes me sick just to think about it.

32

The only reason I can yet suffer this society, is that I am not a part of it.

33

Philosophers cannot really do the work, but they should oversee those who do.

34

There is something profoundly irritating about people who crow, with nothing to crow about.

35

One doesn't know just how blessed one is to be able to play good handball.

36

B.F. Skinner is right, of course.

37

Why are Soviet leaders such windbags?

38

Marjory Stoneman Douglas: "I didn't have any sex life [since 1915]. I've done very well without it, thank you."

A remark like this is almost enough to invalidate all the good work she has done on behalf of the Everglades.

39

Happiness is neither Pleasure nor Victory.

It's both.

40

Jack Valenti of the Motion Picture Association: a more clear, classic, paradigmatic, prototypic case of half-bakedness cannot be found.

41

Genuine peasants and the most preeminent rarefied intellectuals understand one another.

42

Anyone who is not interested in literature is either a slave or a jerk.

43

My book is really an affair between me and God.

44

In the end, the greatest pleasure of my life will have been the perusal of an Atlas.

45

One man's cornerstone is another's footnote.

46

I must confess, the thought of exegeses and critiques and commentaries and controversies and doctoral dissertations and textual comparisons and unearthed notes-and-scribblings and remarkable discoveries of previously unknown preliminary drafts and interviews with friends and associates and the most frivolous and picayune belaborings of my work—

doth really please my vanity.

47

Fernando Lamas with his crooked mouth.

48

If Wayne had stuck by me—page-by-page, line-by-line—mine would have been a more nearly perfect opus.

49

Isn't it interesting how, by a few minimal and deft strokes of the cartoonist's art, a cartoon-strip female can be so extraordinarily (more so than any real-life pose or photograph) ravishing and sexy.

50

Sometimes I like British spellings.

Sometimes I don't.

51

It's criminal for me to work.

52

Wrong as he is about just about everything, Senator Alan Simpson of Wyoming is still a likeable bastard.

53

The now of long-ago was just as now as the now of now.

54

I'm not out of step with the world.

The world is out of step with me.

55

William F. Buckley, Jr. is one of those people who needs to be squashed.

56

What I did experience, I did experience.
What I didn't, I didn't.

There is no way to know anything whatever
about what I didn't.

57

There are so **many** things wrong with Senator Orrin Hatch, I can't even begin to put them all together and tell about them.

58

I know all about Bob Mondello, just from that smug monotoned catty voice alone.

59

With most people, there are no surprises.

60

So few people deserve to have children.

61

One's avocation should be one's vocation.

62

I like Taki's new book.

In fact, as time goes by, I more and more warm up to Taki.

(Except for all that right-wing Bill Buckley nonsense.)

63

Ah, if only I had all of Taki's advantages, and still be me.

64

I'm an expert at not being an expert.

65

That was an uncharitable thing to say about Hume Cronyn-Jessica Tandy.

66

I don't really attack people.

Only personas.

67

I feel differently about different things at different times.

68

No one unit of consciousness (thought, written expression, etc.) can ever be adequate to the Whole.

The realization of this is the beginning of both terror and freedom. And wisdom.

69

An inventor is also a cog, albeit an important one.

70

A saint is simply one who has a personal and existential relationship:

with **everybody**.

71

I have a tendency to over-Capitalize and over-hyphen-ate.

72

I have a tendency to dismiss things (institutions, professions, accents, habits, nationalities, what have you) **wholesale**,

without really **looking** at the infinite variegation of the facts.

73

I like Studs Terkel.

74

I don't want to have to answer to **anybody whatever**.

75

The dictionary is **not** always right.

76

"However good a thing is, it can always be made better."

The knowledge of this very much depresses me.

77

There's a lot of scum out there.

78

Writers are really slaves.

79

Nothing that H. Ross Perot has to say is of any interest to me.

80

When Elvis goes on a postage stamp,

Federal dignity goes out the window.

81

Telling the truth is the Ultimate Game.

82

The best thing about having money,

Is that you don't have to think about money.

83

Wolfe is to Letters, what Mozart is to Music.

84

I resent having anyone over me,

Who isn't smarter than me.

85

There is no way I can have an affair,

With a woman who has a dog.

86

I say again: one can be intelligent and retarded at the same time.

87

There is no way a short-order cook should **ever** have to work more than three hours a day.

88

One of the first things I shall do when I win the lottery, is to call the 1-900 **Hustler** girls and listen to all their dirty talk.

89

I do not, and never did, like basketball.

90

I **still** think Malcolm Muggeridge is a horse's ass.

91

A book written by a young man and edited by that same old one: surely this is a step toward excellence.

92

So many people want to **come** to America.

I've always wanted to get **away** from it.

93

Sometimes I think I am one great big gigantic **ANACHRONISM.**

94

Those who use checks to pay for under-$10 purchases,

Ought to be strung up by the balls or the labia.

95

Experts are there,

To serve their betters.

96

There's a certain inescapable stink about tourism, and a certain inescapable stink about tourists.

97

Everything I've written is embedded in **time**. Therefore nothing I've written can ever be dated, since it is already dated.

98

There is such a thing as being so unprejudiced, that one can afford to be prejudiced.

99

Surely one of the great disappointments of life has to be the betrayal of a friend.

100

No country under the sun has such a stranglehold on cant as does the United States of America.

101

Even in my humility, do I feel a superiority.

102

Nothing more instantly, lightningly, de-sexes me than a tattoo.

103

The Orthodox Observer: a publication more self-serving, drippingly cloying, oh so sweetly proper!, incestuous, insipid, canty... can hardly be found.

104

I can't bear another Fourth of July.

105

Jacksonville is a good place to rest and recuperate between trips.

106

The greatest works of art in our time are the **Nature** series on public television.

107

One can't help anybody when one is down under.

108

At times, **so** many things go wrong, that one just doesn't care anymore.

109

Charlton Heston seems like an intelligent and cultivated man.

110

Andy Dellis knows his languages.

111

H.M. Paduka Seri Baginda Sultan Haji Hassanal Bolkiah Mu'izzadiri Waddaulah is **not** the richest man in the world.

The richest is he who has the most ready money— **and no obligations whatever.**

112

I don't want **POWER.** I want **ENJOYMENT.**

113

I love language,

but I also love things too!

114

Sometimes I think about all those I have scathed and skewered, and the fact that many have children, and that to their children they are fathers and mothers, loved ones,

and I become saddened and wistful and quiet.

115

I hear "Texas," and I bristle.

116

In order to really enjoy sex, you have to have a partner who enjoys it as much as you do.

117

He who would subject himself to the buffoonery of "the political process," is not fit to rule.

118

It is because I love the world so much, that I do not want to be a part of it.

119

Nothing is really incidental.

120

I can't stand a Southern accent on a man, and a Northern one on a woman.

121

I wonder if busboys, short order cooks, toll collectors, bus drivers, factory workers, H.R. Block auditors, theater ushers, and telephone operators also share in the American Dream.

122

Max Lasskow is one hell of a gutsy gritty handball player.

123

How I love the beat and rhythm, brisk good cheer,

Of the pulsing, swinging music of Zaire!

124

It is almost **criminal** for me not to win the lottery.

125

Men **smell** different from women.

126

No one, no writer, philosopher, thinker, seer, mystic, poet—not a one—has ever achieved what T.S. Eliot has achieved.

127

I don't in the least mind teaching, as long as it is on my terms.

128

MY TERMS:

Three hours a week (one course).

Course to be a seminar held on Wednesday evenings from 7 to 10P.M.

One semester (from mid-January to mid-April if in the Northern Hemisphere, mid-June to mid-September if in the Southern).

No more than ten students.

I choose the students (or have veto power over who attends).

I choose the topic(s).

Absolutely no administrative or logistical duties: no advising, committee meetings, faculty meetings, etc.

129

Those who have never been on the brink of suicide, should not be so smug and contemptuous of those who have—

and of those who have gone beyond.

130

I am Nothing.

I am Everything.

131

I am beginning to think of everything-at-once, all-of-the-time.

132

I wish I were a great poet, and could write the definitive poem about two-year-olds.

133

If Eli Bassett is my philosophical Mycroft, Wayne Hamm is my linguistic one.

134

He who has not known Bolivia, hasn't quite lived.

135

All my life I've spent around mostly uninteresting people.

136

Mine is the **LAST FICTION**.

137

    It is indeed rare, most rare, for one Diamond to run across Another.

138

The truth is—you can only imbibe **ONCE** a day.

139

I don't like uppity blacks.

140

Unfortunately, one can also win life's lottery in reverse.

141

One of these days, I'm going to write the truly nasty, smutty, unexpurgated, downright foul and vulgar **Ex Cathedra**.

142

If there's anything I would have liked to know more about—
it is **language**.

143

In the end, the measure of a man is the extent of his goodness.

144

God has yet to prove himself to me, by letting me win the lottery.

145

Cogs don't really know what they're doing;

They just fit into their places.

146

    It's true, and I have to admit it: All healthy children are Aristotelians.

147

    When actors philosophize,

    Something rancid sets in.

148

Golf isn't really such a bad game; it's only the golfers who spoil it.

149

    Why anyone with $100,000,000 would want to be mayor of Los Angeles—is beyond my comprehension.

150

Editors are such shits.

151

To really enjoy a drink, one should be sitting in absolute comfort (with legs propped up), absolutely still, absolutely alone, with perhaps a pipe or hookah, and some Greek/Turkish music in the background.

152

Whenever I see an old beat-up open truck full of pods or watermelons, I invariably think of the **Invasion of the Body Snatchers**.

153

Hot soup (coffee, toddy) should be **hot**.

154

Sometimes I think the only person I can trust is my mother.

155

To all and sundry I say:

Fuck You!

156

I don't like Messianics.

Of any and every persuasion.

157

Unless it turns on itself,

The Body will heal itself,

Provided one waits long enough.

158

There are good cops, and chicken-shit cops.

159

There are times when I suddenly have a **YEN** for blackberries.

Not blueberries or raspberries or loganberries or elderberries, but **blackberries**.

And not supermarket blackberries or canned blackberries or otherwise transported blackberries, but **fresh** blackberries, pulpous and luscious and right off the vine.

Times when I would put up the whole Universe against one basketful of blackberries.

When I would **murder** for my blackberries.

160

No way in hell will I swim in waters where there are any jellyfish around.

161

Andrei Codrescu sitting meekly in the middle seat, while Jay Leno quips with some rock-'n'-roll punk.

Thus it is: the slime and traitorousness of the boot-licking and whoresome intellectual.

162

The tip end of St. Marys, Georgia: one of the last few good places in the U.S.A.

163

I say again: Jimmy Carter is a good man.

164

No one can intimidate me except gourmets and speakers of umpteen languages.

165

I'm a one-book man. And proud of it!

(Poor, confused Tom.)

166

Ksefthelístike, pragmatiká, to Nobel Prize.

167

When I become the Dictator—

Back to the miniskirt.

168

I am the only one I can look up to.

169

Why...why...why...would anyone **LET** himself be interviewed by the likes of Barbara Walters, Howard Stern, Phil Donahue?

170

I've said it time and again that there is no excuse whatever for one not to be deliriously happy provided that:

        a) all of his f-a-c-u-l-t-i-e-s are intact
        b) he has a hefty bank account.

There is, however, one other condition that must obtain, but I dare not mention it.

171

If I were living at an earlier time, I probably would be taking extra good care of my horse.

172

I'm sure they will say about me:

His bark was worse than his bite.

173

There are FRIENDS, and there are Friends, and there are friends.

174

Re **#170**, I'm beginning to realize that some other conditions must obtain as well.

May 12, 1998

Ex Cathedra

11th Encyclical

von Herrn Doktor Professor Peter Joannides

1

    Tommy Hazouri, erstwhile mayor of Jacksonville: whatever his faults, whatever his woes, he did at least get rid of those goddamned toll booths on the Mathews Bridge.

2

Dozing off in a movie house: the sweetest sleep of all.

3

    The thought of my work translated into Japanese—does indeed tickle my vanity.

4

What he says—is not what is wrong with Rush Limbaugh.

5

Gary Cooper as Marco Polo borders on the ridiculous.

6

I have such contempt for professors, because it is they who should be running things,

and they aren't.

7

Orson Welles: a perfect example of the first-and-a-half-rate.

8

Why do most athletic clubs in the U.S.A invariably pipe such shitty music through their every corridor and conduit?

9

One should eat only when ravenously, famishèd-ly hungry.

And not before.

10

I can bear and even forgive rednecks.

But **intellectual** rednecks—that goes beyond the pale.

11

Piano, by itself, is such a bore.

12

I have a weakness and a fondness for syrupy sentimental Hindi musicals, the more syrupy and sugary, the better.

13

Oh no! Spare me, please! Not yet another novelist.

14

I wonder sometimes whether the enlightenment that suddenly descended upon Buddha under the bo tree was simply this: do the best you can under the circumstances.

15

I'm not gay; I just like sex.

16

I guess Patrick Leigh Fermor always was a bit precious, but I didn't really realize it till now.

17

When the English write about Greece, they don't know what the fuck they're talking about.

18

So many writers,

Just diddle with their privates.

19

Cubicles, cubicles. How many millions, billions, spend their lives in cubicles.

20

One should have sex only when ravenously, famishèd-ly horny.

And not before.

21

Neil Postman is a cut above Alvin Toffler.

22

How I love a good seafood dinner after hours and hours of thrashing about in the ocean.

23

I have a profound contempt for just about everybody.

24

John Updike will be remembered more for his critiques than his stories.

25

We forget how wondrous things once were. And that we have an obligation to live and act in equal measure.

26

Of all the televangelists, Fred Copeland has to be the very bottom of the barrel.

27

To all jellyfish, nocuous denizens, and assorted inimical creatures:

You sting; I kill.

28

What sort of person would want to climb the crags of the Acropolis a **second** time?

29

Even from our dearest friends—we sometimes need a little distance.

30

Rid Greece of its motorcycles, motor scooters, mopeds, etc., and I would seriously entertain the notion of living there.

31

Mihalis Lapatsis is in a class by himself.

32

Death puts a different stamp on things.

33

Time puts a different stamp on things.

34

There have been many mini-traditions in my life—if only I had the sense to snatch and savor them while little they lasted.

35

How can one despair of life, so long as:

a) Andean music   b) Greek music   c) Latin music
d) East Indian music exist.

36

Phil Gramm of Texas: the mouther of what is, without a doubt, the most atrocious, ugliest accent in all of senatorial history.

37

John Kerry ought to be the President.

38

Handball players are different from everybody else.

39

Having gone now (periodically—and for several years) to the services of the **American** Catholic Church, I find that one word best describes the proceedings:

insipid.

40

Every meal should be an occasion.

41

Every sexual encounter should be an occasion.

42

I always wanted to pal around with anthropologists.

43

It's a little lonely having no one to look up to except oneself.

44

I'm beginning to **extremely** dislike Senator Phil Gramm of Texas.

(I feel about him the way you would feel about a louse or scorpion suddenly found in our midst, and could easily scrunch and exterminate the son-of-a-bitch without the slightest quiver of conscience.)

45

I don't like Republicans.

46

There are times when a solipsist doesn't think like a solipsist, and times when he does.

47

It's difficult for me to believe that the TIME of the poet has very much to do with the TIME of the physicist.

48

A filet mignon is like a **lokoum**.

49

Nothing more lamebrained than to keep trying to have sex with someone who just isn't interested.

50

It's quite apparent that Joannides has a love/hate relationship to practically everything.

51

Loma de Cabrera: another one (along with Boquete, Keren, Kalimpong, Tafraoute, Ambato, and Cochabamba) of those super-excellent places.

52

I can't work when I'm hungry, and I can't work when I'm stuffed.

53

How often have I lamented: "Great legs! bad bust." "Great bust! bad legs."

54

Only another solipsist can truly understand my work.

55

A rum-and-coke quaffed just after two hard, long, tenacious, gritty, grueling 21-20 games followed by a hard, long, tenacious, gritty, grueling (preferably winning) 11-10 tiebreaker:

It is such startlements that vindicate Existence.

56

One hunk of meat can do the job of a thousand grasses.

57

In emergencies, I'd rather be with Americans than anyone else.

58

Most of our moments and our days are not spent in emergencies.

59

This is no less than the Truth: I want to bed down just about every halfway good-looking woman I see.

60

Eleven games of handball I can play without even the semblance of a strain; but one flight of stairs is sufficient to undo me.

61

Aloneness is good only if it is preceded by a lot of togetherness.

62

There are many different worthinesses of ice cubes: there are the sovereigns of all, hefty chunks that are **sculpted** to increase their cold surface; then there are the hefty chunks that are not sculpted, yet still sturdy and long-lasting; then smaller ones of various and intriguing shapes that can be chewed; then still smaller ones that begin to shade into the unforgivable; and then the unforgivable slivers and flimsy pellets that can turn a drink into instant mush.

63

Young males make me sick; just the sight of them makes me sick.

64

There are some things that even the mighty Nietzsche could not have known about.

Simply because of age.

65

There is something about uniforms—

any uniform...

66

I'm a one-book man, and proud of it!

67

I'm tired of having to **force** my friends to be my friends.

68

Things are looking up: we now have a Spanish (Cuban-Mexican-Dominican-Puerto Rican-Colombian-...) radio station in Jacksonville.

69

There is something obscene about the earnings of certain "entertainers."

Buffoons, popinjays, and harlequins wallowing in the muck of millions of dirty dollars.

70

The time from the first sip of cocktail to the first forkful of food should be exactly one hour and forty-five minutes.

No more; no less.

71

I have finally decided: As much as I would dearly love to (sweet Dubonnet under the warm and lancing sunlight, bittersweet Campari & soda under the warm and lancing sunlight), **THERE IS NO WAY I CAN DRINK IN THE MIDDLE OF THE DAY!**

Unless I am prepared to write off the rest of the day.

72

The camera is wondrous!

The camera is insidious!

73

Patrick Leigh Fermor in his old age: the worst sort of **over**writing that can be imagined, worse even than that of Lawrence Durrell.

74

I could no more write a novel than the man in the moon.

75

Loud noises are **EVIL**.

76

Bad smells are **EVIL**.

77

Whatever I have written,
                        has not been written in stone.

78

I have no qualms about the absolute use of **hopefully**, I spell **forego** in the sense of **give up** or **renounce** with an **e**, and, Nero Wolfe notwithstanding, I shamelessly use **contact** as a verb.

I guess I too must be swept up in the sloppy wave of linguistic change.

79

Frenzy can be spelled either **phrensy** or **frenzy**, and **traveller** with either one **l** or two.

80

Nero Wolfe notwithstanding, I also like a little vinegar on my salad.

81

One can be extremely glib about a subject, and not really know very much about it.

82

To certain asshole critics and editors: We don't all write like Hemingway.

83

I like writers whose output is small.

84

Suppose I **HAD** to choose between Barbara Rush and Laraine Day.

This would be one hell of an agonizing soul-shattering knife-twisting excruciating choice.

85

My work is meant to be (silently but musically) read, not declaimed.

86

Semicolons have no place in a work of literature.

87

Wayne Hamm was the closest thing to genius that I, personally, have ever known.

88

In spite of all my vitriols re American vs. British accents, I'd rather listen, anytime, to the worst Texas redneck drawls or Brooklyn abscesses and obscenities than to the snotty affectations of Diana Rigg.

89

Being able to have sex without having to have children is one of the great breakthroughs of Civilization.

90

I can no more assemble and put up a tent—even a pup tent—than the man in the moon.

91

Nobody profanes Nature so,

like Americans.

92

I know I will have attained to Sainthood,

When I can actually love John Leonard.

93

Oh how I've always wanted to take a shotgun and shoot out the traffic light at Ivey and Southside.

94

I feel about actors the way Mencken used to feel about doctors.

95

One should either tell the whole story, or say nothing at all.

Telling just part of the story can be downright embarrassing.

96

Stereo 90's membership drives,

Drive me up the wall.

97

I don't talk like Henry Fowler, E.B. White, William Strunk, Bob Bryan, or Katharine Hepburn.

I talk like Peter Joannides.

98

David G. McCullough is one of those good Americans.

99

Arianna Stassinopoulos Huffington:

Is she really a Greek?

100

I like Madonna.

101

I feel about doctors the way Mencken used to feel about doctors.

102

I wouldn't mind having a quiet drink with Hal Crowther.

103

What I like to do, nobody pays you for.

104

No greater road maps in all this world than the old Esso road maps.

105

A family is not a real family—unless no less than **two** children are involved.

106

I don't need anyone to tell me that Dos Passos is an important writer.

I have known it all along.

107

Promises won't do, because they cannot take into account the very (and changing) underpinnings of the future.

108

Mihalis taught me to lemonate **marithákia** one at a time.

Otherwise they become soggified.

109

Haiku

Clods in Jacksonville
In the locker room
Talking about football

110

George Will is a much better conversationalist than he is a writer.

111

Papaya is especially good for you. Avocado is especially good for you. The soothing *[cool]* white milk of the coconut is especially good for you.

My instincts tell me this is so.

112

Tyrone Power was the handsomest actor there has ever been.

113

My Seiko quartz wristwatch loses approximately one second every 4-5 days.

I know this because I check it with the Greenwich Mean hourly signal on the BBC, and with the short-wave minute-by-minute signal issuing from Ft. Collins, Colorado.

Each beginning of the month I adjust the 6-8 seconds lost, and every few days I make sure the watch is on course.

Thus, at any given time of day, I can tell you the very **exact** time of day.

114

Intelligence doesn't impress me,

If it isn't coupled with goodness.

115

I don't know how to use computers, word processors, faxes, e-mails, Voice-mails, Webs, Internets.

I am from another, antediluvian, time.

116

I could become really hooked on gummi bears.

117

There's something about a marriage that requires a prenuptial agreement that doesn't sit well with me.

118

I always thought that only the world of professional philosophers had such a huge percentage of snots and snips and freaks and creeps.

But now I know that the world of publishers and editors bats right up there with it.

119

Brown eggs over white.

120

All those cute little essays in **Time** (Charles Krauthammer, Richard Corliss, Lance Morrow, Roger Rosenblatt,...)—smug, clever, isolated, fragmented, in-the-know, name-dropping, read everything and privy to everything, allusion-filled, collusive, full of presumption and hauteur—

just turn my stomach.

121

Mortimer Adler: mostly hot air and blather.

122

Dealing with editors/publishers is like dealing with realtors and car salesmen.

Will be glad when it's over so I can get back to the things that matter, and not to the **vehicles** of the things that matter.

123

I've had it.

With just about everyone.

124

Actors turned authors/philosophers leave me cold.

125

I don't send stamped self-addressed envelopes to **ANYBODY**.

126

What sort of people would build a 65-room 14-bathroom Greek Revival mansion on the banks of the Hudson, replete with floral sways, balustrades, and pilasters, Italian marbles and Flemish tapestries, oak panelings and gilded Louis XIV designs, baroque and rococo extravagances and Greek vessels, with no less than 24 servants in attendance, and formal portraits of ancestors on the walls?

Jesus!

127

I'm glad I don't live in the 19th century and have to smell horse manure all the time.

128

All women have a fuckability index ranging from 0-10:

0's abound
1-4's abound
5-7's are surprisingly and delightfully numerous
8's are rare (but not all that rare, in absolute terms)
9's are **extremely** rare
10's are practically non-existent

129

To certain latter-day rock-bottom black stand-up comedians:

Sordidissimi de sordidis.
(You're no Richard Pryor, assholes.)

130

I had no idea that Charles Krauthammer is a paraplegic.

131

Thomas Sowell: Thou dost protest a bit too much.

132

I must confess—even in this age of human rights, affirmative actions, rainbow coalitions, international protocols, ethnic exaltations—I still would have enjoyed being a **bwana**.

133

WAPE Radio, Jacksonville: the shit music on the all-shit station.

134

Some books are **firefly** books: that is, flashes of wit, perceptiveness, and incandescence punctuated by sometimes long intervals of incoherence and unintelligibility.

But perhaps such books ought to be published. After all, one can't have the flashes without the darkness.

135

I don't **feel** like a senior citizen.

136

The lists in my work. The long, sometimes excessive and wearying lists.

I have **earned** the right to have them.

DOCTOR Laura Schlessinger (and others like her—all of her ilk):

Instant, impudent, plastic psychological wisdom dispensed to all the call-in waiting-with-bated-breath retards.

138

John Updike on Robert Benchley

As much as I like and respect Updike, he should not, I think, patronize his betters.

139

All those featherweight talk-show philosophers.

140

People who appear on panels and talk shows are (no matter how old) adolescents.

141

    I wouldn't trade my early early childhood with anybody's on earth.

142

    I no longer want a Rolex. I am content with a Seiko.

    Provided I can replace it at the slightest imperfection.

143

    People who give lectures and write books are (no matter how old) adolescents.

144

    Pancakes do **not** take the place of toast.

145

    English announcers (especially females) on American radio stations—
        are just too snooty for words.

146

    God created the lion to devour the lamb,

    And me to squilch and dispatch cockroaches.

147

    Chicken livers—prepared with flair, painstaking care—are one of the culinary epiphanies of our civilization.

148

    The super-excellent places actually now number nine: Tafraoute, Keren, Swat, Boquete, Cochabamba, Kalimpong, Loma de Cabrera, Ambato, and Salta.

    Nine locations; nine sovereign nations.

149

    If I **have** to be reincarnated—

          let it be as an otter.

150

    All these principled actions, moral incorruptibilities, artistic integrities, sacrificial self-denials, unswerving loyalties, courageous stances—

    Next to a true physical illness, they are nothing but child's play.

151

    An orthodoxly religious stance indicates a certain feebleness of mind.

152

    Ever since it was reported that Demi Moore had implants—

          it never again can be the same.

153

Aching joints make for metaphysical gloom.

154

It is not things, but experiences, that one should amass.

155

Some of those Forbes billionaires remind me of weasels.

Especially the Asiatic ones.

156

Not all car salesmen are like car salesmen.

157

An eggplant is not an eggplant. Nor is it a **melintzána**.

It is an **AUBERGINE**.

This is its rightful name.

158

No people age more gracelessly than Americans.

159

What makes doctors think their time is more valuable than mine?

160

Live long enough,

And see some of your most cherished certainties go tumbling out the window.

161

There's no way a great writer can also be a diplomat.

I never did take to George Seferis.

A priori.

162

Why do I—nude except for a pair of slippers—look so ridiculous?

163

I have probably lived the good life all along, and never realized it.

164

What is the best thing about France? The best thing about France is this:

The wondrous cheeses reeled in on a tray at mealdom's end.

165

One who would deliberately and casually throw his chewing gum onto a pavement for others to step on, get all over their shoes, inside their cars, within their homes, into their rugs, onto their floors...

ought to have his face beaten to a bloody pulp.

166

I do my own editing.

167

AM Radio: My God! It has to be heard to be believed! A whole new seething clodhopping low-life Underworld.

In fact, quite entertaining.

168

Nothing in the Universe cools as quickly as a baked potato.

169

The most sophomoric and embarrassing sort of fiction is that which recreates actual historical personalities.

170

There's something about making a **fetish** of music—

that really turns me off.

171

After all these years, beginning to realize that maybe Phil Silvers wasn't such a bad guy after all.

172

I am mellowing.

173

Fireworks have never impressed me.

174

Creams over ointments.

175

    Sections of the morning paper in order of precedence and importance:

lottery results
international news
jumble (word puzzle)
metro news
arts and social events
neighborhood news
sports
financial section
classifieds and advertisements

176

It amuses me to think of the lordly Vanderbilts, during the early years of the century, looking supremely and haughtily down from their lofty Biltmore, and having not an inkling that a young boy in the town below would achieve a significance and a worth greater than all their treasures and millions put together.

177

A great comic routine:

Magnificent when it is done once.

Something wrong when it is done twice.

178

The greatest onomatopoeia of all literature: Wolfe's depiction of a rushing galloping train.

179

Why is it that—

Things that were crystal clear to me just moments ago,

Become so tortuous and murky when I try to **explain** them?

180

National Public Radio: National Jewish Radio

181

James Carville: Bad News

182

Sometimes, and in its own way, I'm even tempted to consider it a **great** film: **The Day the Fish Came Out**.

183

Bad food diminishes the soul,

And upsets the stomach.

184

The genuinely friendliest Americans are probably Montanans.

185

Greece and its mopeds; America and its dogs.

186

I have a lurking suspicion that, in some significant way, it is not good not to eat meat.

187

WAPE Radio: Jacksonville.

I absolutely **HATE** that fucking station.

188

Having breakfast at Steffen's Restaurant in Kingsland, Georgia—excellent ham, eggs over-medium-medium-well, home fries, toast, pancake, strawberry jam, loads and loads of coffee—is pure bliss.

189

I do sometimes speak ill of the dead.

May 19, 2000

Ex Cathedra

12th Encyclical

von Herrn Doktor Professor Peter Joannides

1

What ever insidious thing did happen to that once peaches-and-cream gal, Jane Pauley?

2

I'm getting sick and tired of those who live and work in New York City.

I'm sick of their busyness, abruptness, un-courtliness, ill-manneredness, churlishness, inconsiderateness.

May they all fry in hell.

3

I believe in love at first sight.

4

I love women,
                    but I can't stand all the trouble I have to go through to have them.

5

The most overrated actor of Hollywood: Clint Eastwood.

6

Why has my soul so wholly appropriated the song **Mas**?

Why does it so beguilingly call to mind roads I did not take, lives I did not lead, lovers hypothetical, dimensions impalpable, mysteries unfathomable, alternate universes?

7

One can be very very intelligent and still be a peasant.

8

Every once in a while, I get an absolute **YEN** for it. I can rearrange my schedule for it; suffer hours and hours of hunger for it; lie, cheat, steal, murder for it; drive 75 miles out of my way for it:

An Arby's Beef and Cheddar Sandwich, with curly fries, Coke, and Horsey Sauce.

9

Exactly the same thing happens with:

A plate of **hummus** ladled with olive oil and kalamata olives—and sheaves of pita bread to dip into it with.

10

How many times a day do I, under my breath, utter the word **Merde!** (in English)—

at least 20-30 times, I would say.

11

Assorted whores, clowns, windbags, gorgons, and loonies:

Alan Dershowitz   Robert Tilton
Johnny Cochran   Marcia Clark
F. Lee Bailey   Rod Parsley
Susan Estrich   Barbara de Angelis
James Carville   Joyce Meyer
Susan Pewter   Kenneth Copeland

12

Roman antiquities bore me to tears.

13

All the technology, impersonality, compartmentalization, isolation, grindingness, anomie of modern life—still cannot destroy the humanity of Italy.

14

I don't see what Europeans see in American films.

15

Greek antiquities bore me to tears.

16

Greek bees are a pain in the ass.

17

The one-handed hand-held European shower is just plain stupid.

18

Nobody eats like Mihalis Lapatsis. And family. And friends.

19

Everything is getting old, fast.

20

From everything I've said, it's pretty obvious that I would like Holland more than Belgium.

21

Anyone who wouldn't place Wolfe's work in the top 100 English-speaking novels of the 20th Century is full of shit.

22

I tend to agree with Ford's infamous pronouncement on History.

23

A good word for the French: slimes.

24

Afghanistan wins, hands down, the very highest honors.

Even over Benin and the formidable Honduras.

25

My Kingdom for a new pair of knees!

26

Hilton Head, South Carolina:

Oh how neat and tidy, so groomed and color-coded and well-apportioned—

and so depressing.

27

After a stroke, one is never the same.

28

Reader's Digest—"It pays to increase your word power."

I invariably miss one or two,

And this infuriates me.

29

Money, generally, is in the wrong hands.

30

Phrases I can no longer abide:

"The Founding Fathers," "The American People," "The American Dream," "the bottom line," "where he's coming from," "target audience," "unilateral," "bilateral," "at this point in time," "very unique."

31

All Americans, myself included, have (at the very least) a touch of kookiness about them.

32

A good Brie restores my faith in the Universe.

33

There is exaggeration and distortion in practically everything I say.

But there is also a measure of truth in everything I say.

34

Why would anyone want a different cut of steak, when he could have filet mignon?

35

I'm not a run-of-the-mill solipsist.

I'm a sophisticated solipsist.

36

Black Republicans: an anomaly, and somewhat distasteful.

37

Bryant Gumbel: a chemically pure case of hubris.

38

Why would anyone who could write **The Kandy-Kolored Tangerine-Flake Streamline Baby** and **The Electric Kool-Aid Acid Test**—then go on to do plotty figmental **novels**?!

This is beyond my comprehension.

39

The sultry Rita Hayworth never did anything for me.

And neither did Marilyn Monroe and Lana Turner and Ava Gardner.

On the other hand...there was Paulette Goddard and Virginia Mayo and Olga San Juan and Ann Rutherford and Susan Hayward and Joan Bennett and Arlene Dahl and Hedy Lamarr and Linda Darnell and Eleanor Parker and Gloria DeHaven and Ruth Roman and Silvana Mangano and Gina Lollobrigida and Ann Miller and Mitzi Gaynor.

40

There is no way an actor can be a first-rate individual.

41

Was it Gore Vidal who said that anyone who would read from his own work in a public forum is nothing less than a pompous nerd?

I heartily second the thought.

42

There will come a time when nobody will read novels any longer.

43

When it comes to matters of the highest import:

Clarity is no match for Vagueness.

44

It must be nice for John Updike to have **The New Yorker** at his beck and call.

45

The measure of a man is the extent to which he subverts his predictability.

46

I love Arabs; I don't much like Muslims.

47

I speak, write, read, and think in English,

But English is not my language.

48

Health
Friendship
Money

in that order

49

Whenever someone happens to get to a waiting queue just seconds before I do, I have this irresistible urge to grab him or her by the throat and kick him or her in the ass just as hard as I can.

50

Senator Robert Byrd of West Virginia: a historicitous gasbag.

51

I've noticed that every time I go travelling, something is always hurting and spoiling: an itchy rash, an unlanced boil, a stomped heel, an inflamed knee, a feverous blister, a strained shoulder, a sore gum, what have you.

52

To denigrate a whole country (Mexico)—with its rich and varied heritage of music and culture and language and custom—on the basis of a few unfortunate encounters, is nothing less than asinine.

This applies to the author of **Ex Cathedra, 6th Encyclical (#61),** *Amán Amán!* as well. (The Mexican part.)

53

Mexican antiquities pretty much bore me to tears.

54

It's beginning to dawn upon me that personality type is a far more accurate divider of reality than any national or linguistic conformity.

55

When I hear those Andean flutes, it is like God Himself calling.

56

I don't like Caribbean lounge lizards: indolent, flatulent, full-of-fluff, time-murdering, posturing, hubristic, wise-ass American expatriates.

57

Técun Umán, Guatemala: a bit of hell on earth.

58

What good is a country—despite its rich and varied heritage of music and culture and language and custom—if it always gives you the trots.

59

As I drive my car, there are times when I think of myself as **slicing** through the myriad structures—**slicing slicing** through the thick matted concatenated interwattled intermixtured conmixtured mottle and bounty of structures.

Just like on the train from Cape Charles to Penn Station.

60

Anyone who has been through the mill and terror of a hospital should know how vulnerable we all are.

And should no longer be full of a blusterous ego.

61

I like the rhythm, delivery, thoughts, and sentiments of George Carlin.

But then I think of his routine being done again and again and again and again.

(As in a stint in Las Vegas.)

And I get a bad taste in my mouth.

62

I detest dogs.

Of all varieties.

63

Paris and dog shit.

64

Bad Krozingen, Germany:

Here no tourists, no hoopla, no art museums, no hangers-on, no interpreters, no come-ons, no historicities, no picturesqueness, no national treasures, no self-consciousness.

Just a good solid German town, where people work, love, die, quarrel, go to school, shop at the butcher's, sweep the sidewalk in the morning hours, have a beer and a schnitzel at the local hotel on a Thursday night.

Well worth a visit.

65

How I hate Sundays and Holidays!

When all the shops are closed.

66

Hilaire Belloc must have been everything I would have detested, and do detest.

67

I have great respect for breakthrough scientists and auto mechanics.

68

I love porno films—the more pornicious, the better.

69

Aside from matters of health,

There are few things that could not be put right by winning the lottery.

70

Anything less than winning the lottery (the **BIG** lottery, that is) just doesn't interest me any more.

71

    Romans in cinematic spectaculars declaiming with British accents—

        makes me want to puke.

72

    He who fucks with Wolfe (or Verne, Nietzsche, Wells, Logan Pearsall) fucks with me.

73

    It hilariously gets me that Hemingway really did think highly of himself.

74

    Doris Day and Rock Hudson—

        clicked.

75

If ever I **do** win the lottery—

WATCH OUT!

76

I'm glad I did all my philandering before it became so heinous for supervisors to compliment their secretaries and teachers to date their students.

77

Ayn Rand: another first-and-a-half rater.

78

Prolific writers are inferior writers.

79

What is it about the Benchley drawings of Gluyas Williams that can transport me, as if by some instant chemical magic, to some earlier and halcyon, Proustian-pure unblemished time?

80

The most interesting subject matter I can think of:

Myself.

81

I somehow wish I could have been there during the two World Wars, when thousands were asked to spill their guts in foul-rotted trenches and bloodied fields, trying to kill their counterparts as miserable and terror-stricken as themselves, to somehow been in a position to tell one and all to shove it right up Foch's and Hindenberg's and Pershing's and Montgomery's and Rommel's and von Paulus's and Patton's and Eisenhower's uniformed ass.

82

The two most intense pleasures of life:

A terribly terribly illicit sexual happening when deprived for a long long time.

A glass of cool cool water when terribly terribly thirsty.

83

The following are true propositions:

Everything that happened had to happen exactly as it did happen and couldn't have happened any other way.

There is no justice in nature. The good are sometimes felled and the bad rewarded.

Catastrophes and upheavals are icily indifferent to whoever gets in their way.

No miracles have ever occurred.

The planet can be obliterated by a collision with another celestial object.

It is possible for a viral strain or other biological quirk to obliterate the human species.

84

There is no God, unless what is meant is an advanced extraterrestrial, if any.

85

The true madness is **not** being a solipsist.

86

Acting is a despicable profession.

Even though it can sometimes be instrumental in effecting something of value.

87

I have so many prejudices that they cancel one another out.

88

Stephen Jay Gould: The Encyclopaedic Man!

89

I want to find someone exactly like myself who is not exactly like myself.

90

No editor will get his dirty hands on a single word of what I've written.

91

I don't work at **Ex Cathedra** lines; they just happen.

92

Spare me, please, from wonderful editors like Bob Gottlieb, Michael Korda, and Jonathan Galassi.

93

THE GRASSHOPPER AND THE ANTS

I'm the grasshopper.

I had a lot of fun.

94

If I were a child, I'd hiss and spit at Mr. Rogers.

95

I don't like the **look** of Thomas Mann.

96

It's hard to believe that my vision of the world will go with me when I go.

97

I like to step on lots of to-be-stepped-on-deserving toes.

98

I hope I never see another classroom as long as I live.

99

Now that travel is no longer a frontier, I guess the only one left is that of sex.

100

I don't want to be President or a CEO or an Ambassador or a General or an expert or a concert pianist or an eminent surgeon or a movie star or a renowned scientist or a tennis champion or a Chairman of the Board or a college administrator or a publishing mogul or a celebrity writer or a stock-market wizard...

I just want to be a healthy anonymous billionaire.

101

John Updike is beginning to get a bit too encyclopaedy for my taste.

102

For a very very select few, there comes a time, and a sudden realization, that "More of the Same" is no longer acceptable,

And off they go in a startlingly new direction.

103

You just **know** that collard greens are good for you.

104

Winning the lottery in reverse: airplane crashes, train collisions, freak accidents, rare diseases, shark attacks, lightning strikes, tornado whirls, mudslides.

105

It constantly amazes me how most people can blithely go about their business without screamingly lamenting not being terribly rich.

106

The trouble with John Updike is that his writing, although highly and exquisitely polished, lacks the **eccentricity** and **idiosyncrasy** that the shape of his head and the look of his face intimate.

107

When I read History, I have to have Pictures.

108

If I had won the lottery early on, I probably would have turned into, God forbid, a Donald Trump.

109

It pleased me:

When Truman fired MacArthur.

110

Augmented breasts are like toupees: easy to spot.

111

In all this welter of processed ash—pawed over by editors, sub-editors, line-editors, layout-experts, jacket-designers, spell-checkers, blurb-writers—I hope there will be a someone who will appreciate a strictly and vehemently handmade product.

112

Given the wonders of childhood,

One has no right to become jaded.

113

In shops, restaurants, bars, airplanes, ticket counters, department stores, information booths...

I prefer to be waited on by women, not men.

November/December 1999

    There's a certain Miss on one of those early morning television exercise shows—exquisitely well-proportioned, round and jiggling and ample and thrusting—

    that is driving me salivatingly crazy.

115

    A perfectly contoured breast—of just the right fullness and angle and taper—

    is a thing of beauty and a joy forever.

116

    Any dismemberment of my work—any quotation, excision, isolation, fragmentation—dislodged and wrenched from its rightful place in the reach and flow of the Whole—would be a gross misrepresentation.

117

Life is like a round of poker. A certain amount of skill and gumption is involved in playing the game,

> but not all that much.

118

Writers whose introductions to other writers' works are almost as long as, and sometimes longer than, the very works they are introducing—are jerks.

119

I rather enjoy playing the part of **enfant terrible**.

120

I could have sworn Merv Griffin was Jewish.

121

David Hume:

"I am apt to suspect the Negroes and in general all other species of men (for there are four or five different kinds) to be naturally inferior to the whites. There never was a civilized nation of any other complexion than white, nor even any individual eminent either in action or speculation. No ingenious manufacturers amongst them, no arts, no sciences."

How a great philosopher, and perhaps one of the greatest of philosophers, could have written anything so inordinately stupid only shows the sometimes enormous **unevenness** of human beings.

122

O Theós is not the same as God.

123

Few could have intimidated me; but Noel Coward would have been one of them.

124

What did one really know at the age of seven? At fourteen? At thirty-one? At forty-five?

What does one really know now?

125

There's a certain restaurant in Brussels that serves the most excellent pizza imaginable.

126

The essence of sex is illicitness.

127

If I were living in Revolutionary Times, it's quite possible that I would have been a Loyalist.

Some additional (see previous **Ex Cathedras**, and assorted other sections of *Amán Amán!*) excellent and noteworthy films:

The Asphalt Jungle	The Wrong Man
The Flight of the Phoenix	An Affair to Remember*
Shirley Valentine	Pillow Talk*
The Desperate Hours	The Treasure of the Sierra Madre

(continued)

128-A

It Happened One Night	Tobacco Road
Drive a Crooked Road	Only Angels Have Wings
Zorba, the Greek	Rebecca
Mr. Smith Goes to Washington	Dial M For Murder
	Key Largo
Z	Moulin Rouge
Amarcord	The Long Voyage Home
On the Waterfront	The Bridge on the River Kwai
The Quiet Man	

(continued)

128-B

Sayonara*
Picnic
Who's Afraid of Virginia Woolf?
They Drive By Night
Shane
Double Indemnity
The Lost Weekend

Roman Holiday
The Lavender Hill Mob
Airport
Tugboat Annie
Separate Tables
Ruggles of Red Gap
5 Fingers

(continued)

128-C

Cat Ballou
Topkapi
Hell in the Pacific
The Hustler
Strangers When We Meet
The Adventures of Robinson Crusoe
Cyrano de Bergerac

The Thin Man
Devil in the Flesh
The Shoes of the Fisherman
The Man Who Could Work Miracles
The Party
The Naked Prey
Woman's World

* in hindsight

129

Andy Rooney is no Benchley.

But sometimes he comes close.

And he is certainly head and shoulders above all other Pretenders.

130

Even if I were a billionaire, I wouldn't want any servants.

131

The essential purpose of a clock/wristwatch is to tell time as accurately as possible.

Thus, the most elaborate and ornate mechanical movement is inferior to the lowliest quartz.

132

Every endeavor of the arts other than solitary writing is a bit crass.

133

Andy Rooney is one of those good Americans.

134

Celebrities (and even unknown actors) who hawk commercials are morally putrid.

135

With regard to any Greek-American Orthodox ceremony, words and intonations in Greek ring true; in English, false (and ridiculous).

136

Having recently seen one of his later films, I'm no longer sure of **entry 5**.

137

If times were jumbled, and the early and impressionable were to be reversed with the later and impermeable, entry 129 might have read like this:

Robert Benchley is no Rooney.

But sometimes...

138

Even when I disagree with Andy Rooney (for example, about dogs), I still like Andy Rooney.

139

The most underrated writer of our time: Andy Rooney.

140

Here I am, after having promised myself to no longer waste my time reading fiction, captivated by the stories of Jhumpa Lahiri.

141

There **ARE** such things as free lunches: for Inheritors and Lotto Winners.

142

The **CLEAN LINE** takes in Germany, Austria, Switzerland, Holland, Denmark, Norway, Sweden, Finland (and perhaps Very Northern Italy, Slovenia, Iceland, and New Zealand).

Any place on the other side of that line is, at best, a bit **sucio**.

143

Most reapers of handicap stickers don't look handicapped to me.

144

I wonder if there is such a thing as genuine friendship in the United States of America?

145

If I had to be an expert on something, I guess I would choose:

    a) wildflowers
    b) liquor bottles
    c) cheeses
    d) small friendly hotels (worldwide)
    e) erotogenic places, nuances, and acts

146

If it were up to me, I would have it be:

Lifelong friends with all my ex-lovers.

147

    I've always wanted to have a handball court, built on stilts, over Caribbean or Aegean waters, with a trapdoor, so that right after a 21-20, 20-21, 11-10 (preferably winning) match, I could plop right into the ocean.

148

I see it everywhere. I see it rampant:

Intelligence without sensitivity.
Intelligence without dependability.
Intelligence without moral fibre.

Intelligence without awareness.

149

God help me from ever owning a Mustang. And I also don't want a mini Fiat, a Ford Escort, a Town Car, a Cadillac, a Rolls Royce, or a Lamborghini.

A Toyota Camry or Lexus 300 will do me fine.

150

I don't want just one or two lovers. I want scores and scores of them.

151

Ickycutesysnobbysaccharineypoo: Nancy Novogrod's opening monthly blurb in "Travel & Leisure."

152

Arugula has no less than a mystic taste.

153

Some things I can eat and eat and eat, on and on and on, a source of never ending savor, of which I never seem to tire:

Apricots (plump and soggy, just about to let go from the tree), mango, papaya (plump and red and chilled), scallops, oysters, shrimp, crème caramel, brie, blackberries, figs (plump and soggy, just about to let go from the tree), clam chowder.

154

I, for one, don't see what's so great about the poem "Howl."

155

The Department of Street Maintenance and Repairs of the City of Jacksonville shows me absolutely nothing.

156

Another phrase I can no longer abide: "to send (him, her, them, it) a message."

157

Another noteworthy film: **Bye Bye Love**.

158

More bad news: Representative Tom DeLay of Texas.

159

One of the most electrifying lines/scenes of all moviedom. From the original **Lost Horizon**:

"My name is Chang."

160

One yearns to speak French—not for France, but for the former French colonies.

161

Interesting places I yet long to visit: Novaya Zemlya, Port Blair, Torres del Paine, the Laccadives, Bhutan, Oman, Kastellorizon, Limnos, Imbros, Nouakchott, Van, Inoucdjouac, Cocos, Bouvet Island, Clipperton Island, Chagos Archipelago, Sala y Gómez, Maria Theresa Reef (Île Tabor).

162

I say again: there are good cops and there are chicken-shit cops.

July 11, 2001

Ex Cathedra

13th Encyclical

von Herrn Doktor Professor Peter Joannides

1

Some episodes of **Emmanuelle** were excellent. Especially the one that takes place in Hong Kong.

2

Fruit should be enjoyed when one is good and hot and thirsty and hungry,

> not **after** a belly-bloating meal.

3

What is it about **Casablanca** that makes it such a special special film?

Why is it that no matter how many times to it exposed, I sit riveted riveted, daring not to miss a single scene, until the very end?

4

The Great American Novel may have been written (Dos Passos); but The Great Earth-an Novel has yet to be.

in Greece

5

One way to meet interesting people is to stay at small hotels.

6

Air conditioning is not a luxury; it is a scorching, succouring, soul-saving necessity.

7

Sometimes I think Turks are more decent than Greeks.

8

Actors are hams, the world over.

9

In Greece, look to the mountains, not the seashore, to find the sylphs and whispers that are rapidly disappearing.

10

Ninetta always used to say, "If only the Swiss had Greece..."

After all these many years, I am beginning to understand what she meant.

11

No matter how small the library, no matter how wayside the town,

Something—at least one thing—of surprising and inordinate interest will invariably make its appearance.

12

A very little thing can sometimes make a whole lot of difference.

(E.g., a screen, a fan, a can opener, a flashlight, a pair of pliers, a washer, a scotch tape, a piece of string, a rubber band, a sponge, a safety pin, a spoon.)

13

It's a shame one can't be Everywhere,

In September/October.

14

Most people are peasants.

15

The loose ends will never be tied up.

16

What some feel about Shakespeare, I feel about Wolfe.

17

Hermann Hesse's review of **Look Homeward, Angel** ratcheted him up about ten notches.

18

(Most) Greek-American girls have a certain stink about them, sort of like tourists and philosophy professors.

19

You could do a lot worse than be a Greek.

20

The little fishes in Greece make it all worthwhile.

21

Nero and I: from the same part of the world.

22

Sometimes I get the greatest high from a glass of plain cold water.

23

I'm getting sick and tired of being told how **old** Greek civilization is.

24

For me, trips can no longer start at 6 A.M.

25

There's something crass about having that glitzy restaurant in the Eiffel Tower named after my beloved author.

26

If I were running things, I'd throw every last screeching, roaring, ear-splitting, mufflerless son-of-a-bitch motorcyclist/motorscooterist in a dank and rotting jail.

27

Although I love it when somehow pictures have been taken, hardly ever is it I who take any pictures.

28

I hate Sundays.

29

If I had to choose another language to speak, on the basis of pure pleasure alone, it would have to be Italian.

30

I've never really met anyone like myself.

31

He who doesn't drink,

Lives in sin.

32

Lynchers ought to be lynched.

33

It's the **intellectual** New Yorkers that I don't like.

34

History begins with Photographs,

And not before.

35

I really think someone should write that science fiction tale of one suddenly gifted (by the aliens) to speak every language and every dialect on the planet, fluently.

36

Priests, Archbishops, Patriarchs, monks, missionaries—even of an unfanatical, ornate, and colorful persuasion such as Orthodoxy—are wearing thin.

37

In and out the tourists come and go,
Talking of Michelangelo,

Having hardly a wisp of an idea begun,
Of what in town is really going on.

38

I don't, **generally**, like taxi drivers.

39

The worst thing about Greece: its mufflerless (something that could be corrected and whose prohibition could be **enforced**) motorcycles, motor scooters, mopeds, etc.

The best thing about Greece: its music and songs.

40

There's something terribly cozy about living in a **retiré** (ρετιρέ).

41

God! how I hate the mannerisms of professors:

The pregnant little pauses, the patronizing jocularities, the "regular guy"/penetrating intellectual poses, the vast fund of knowledge and expertise of which said experts deign to dispense some breathless modicum, the knowing nods and nays and looks, the theatricalities, the name-dropping, the self-importance, the sickly pride, the hubris, the smug innuendoes, the little circus performance for their captive audience...

I spit on professors.

42

People who give speeches to more than ten individuals are retarded.

43

Philosophy over the centuries has spawned more prime-grade bullshit than you can shake a stick at.

44

There are Greek theosophists, Greek spiritualists, Greek mediums, Greek vegetarians, Greek Buddhists, Greek astrology-lovers, Greek yoga-worshippers, Greek windbags, Greek bores, Greek loonies, Greek smart-asses, Greek jerks, Greek jackasses, Greek assholes...

Just like anyplace else.

45

A terribly personal/topical/private/idiosyncratic entry, with apologies to the general reader:

The little snotty runt, Georgos Polyhroniou, reminds me of Ayn Rand's Ellsworth Toohey.

46

WASPy Texas Republicans: ugly stances, ugly sentiments, ugly twangs, ugly souls, ugly people.

WASPy Texas Republicans: Texas shit.

47

In my youth, I was anti-American, anti-German, pro-Greek, pro-Italian, and pro-English.

In my near-old age, I am not-so-anti-American, not-so-**so**-pro-Greek, pro-German, pro-Italian, pro-Turkish, pro-Arab, anti-French, and anti-Afghani.

In my old age, I will be...

48

WASPy Alabama/Mississippi Republicans:

Alabama/ Mississippi shit.

49

I just can't get over how **different** siblings can be.

50

WASPy Florida Republicans:

more Southern shit.

51

The U.S. Presidential election of 2000:

A more clear-cut example of Hume's "Reason is the slave of the passions" cannot be found.

52

The U.S. Presidential election of 2000:

Didn't you just **know** that that courtly and gentlemanly Chief Justice of the Florida Supreme Court would vote against Gore.

53

Early morning chummy, familiar, blathering, music-interrupting radio disc jockeys really turn me off.

54

The (American) wit and repartee of Archie Goodwin has yet to be equaled.

55

Why anyone would be terribly interested in anything other than food, sex, sport, music, beauty, travel, and good conversation is certainly beyond me.

56

I'd like to collect every last stray dog on this planet—

and make perfumed soap out of them.

57

Greek priests are beginning to remind me of African shamans and New Guinea bone-through-the-nosers.

58

Urban Greece: There are times when I feel as if I've been suddenly dumped onto one of those Balkan countrylings where, by some fluke, I just happen to speak the local language.

59

I'm amused at all these glowing obituaries for all sorts of undeserving demagogues, fakers, third raters, mountebanks, frauds, bores, buffoons, academic popinjays and cock-a-doodle-doos.

60

Religious people are often bad people.

61

I'm still an old Newtonian—Einstein, Heisenberg, Planck, et al. notwithstanding.

62

American musical crap with Greek lyrics: it turns my stomach.

63

The literary sensibility is the highest kind.

64

They who do commercials are whores.

65

One thing I don't need is to appear on television.

66

Soccer is slowly becoming one colossal bore.

67

What a letdown!

To realize that in Greece I'm just another "Pete Johnson."

68

Certain disciplines engender a sort of secret and proprietary pride—that of the cosmologist, the astronomer, the physicist, the psychologist, the psychiatrist, the economist, the physiologist, the mathematician.

Each one imagines himself as the core provider. Each one thinks of himself as in some sense **subsuming** the others.

They are, of course, all wrong.

The only legitimate pride is that of the literary philosopher.

69

Bad odors are as much of an excruciating pain as any tactile happening.

70

The trouble with America is that, in spite of its vaunted multiformity, it is really unidimensional.

71

To **eat** with someone, to share a meal, to break bread together—is one of the great inroads to friendship and intimacy.

72

The only music that **supervenes**—that dares supervene—over Greek music is that of the High Andes.

73

The more President Clinton was involved in sexual dalliance, the more I respected him.

74

I don't see that **how** music is made need be of any especial interest to a lover of music.

(Any more so than that a ship's captain need have an intimate knowledge of the boiler room below.

Or a gourmet, the details and workings of the cooks and help in the kitchen.)

75

Going to a concert is stultifying.

76

Music is best on the run.

77

In case one didn't get it:

Music-makers are to music-lovers as slaves are to masters.

78

...with apologies once again:

Aliki Vouyouklaki wasn't really as sugary-sentimental as I thought.

79

It's hard for me to believe that other languages are as complex as this elaborate entangled maddening intimidating labyrinthine self-feeding self-perpetuating ever-accruing ever-yeasting forever-ramifying Greek.

80

One whole small bottle of CAIR retsina before lunch:

this now become a sacrosanct tradition.

81

I know there must be some few others like me, but only God knows who and where they are.

82

Quite some time ago, I came across a story by Allen Ginsberg about a man at a party where happenings were simultaneously described in two simultaneous dimensions.

I thought it was one of the most brilliant pieces of writing I had ever encountered.

83

The intensity of a sexual experience is directly proportional to the longevity of its absence.

84

Sexual perversion can be a sign of intelligence, health, and superiority.

85

The **view**'s the thing.

86

The most memorable and intriguing dance I've ever seen was that of the seven-foot warriors in **King Solomon's Mines**.

87

Economics is a bore.

88

Wittgenstein's **Philosophical Investigations** in Greek!

This a little bit blows my mind.

89

T.S. Eliot's **Four Quartets** in Greek.

This soothes and gladdens my mind and heart.

90

I cannot resist an entry entirely the property of my good friend R.B.:

> Somebody told me recently that Nostradamus is interpreted as claiming that in this year the greatest nation on earth would select as its leader the village idiot.

And so it has come to pass.

91

The planet is becoming exhilaratingly, stupefyingly, unfortunately, irreversibly one.

92

The secret of Mediterranean warmth and humanity is the climate/happy childhood.

93

I loathe dogs; I respect wolves.

94

Apothegms cannot be explained.

95

People: hardly ever other than twisted, callous, or limited.

96

"I'm so glad I was born a man and not a dog."

What does this really mean?

Oh wouldn't Wittgenstein have a field day with this!

97

I can't stand cheery adult goody-goodies who sweetly communicate with children.

98

For Paul Newman, for whom I have considerable respect:

Why anyone would risk death or deformity racing cars or climbing precipitous mountains—while food, drink, sex, libraries, travel, friendship, stimulating conversation, wildflowers, handball games, childhood memories, belly laughs, epiphanies await to be savored—simply doesn't make sense to me.

99

There's no end to knowledge, so there comes a time when one just has to level off.

100

Eating cucumbers—except for highly specialized circumstances (such as, as an accompaniment to **oúzo**)—is like eating hay.

101

I exercise so I can enjoy my drink.

102

Alas! Beloved Typewriter.

Farewell.

103

95% of Greek songs are about eros and love.

And so it should be.

104

There's a sense in which tasteful hard-core pornography is way ahead of its time.

105

...with apologies, for the last time:

If anyone deserves more the epithets "gorgon" and "bitch," it's that pompous, theatrical, self-promoting, constantly-interrupting, know-it-all, phony, familiar, disrespectful, patronizing television hostess Vicky Flessa.

It's a shame that she's also such a beautiful woman.

106

What makes disc jockeys think that anyone is in the least bit interested in their wit, opinions, and prattle?

107

What I really really want is one of those ravishing well-bronzed Brazilian humping-bumping-twisting Carnival nympho-sexpots.

108

From time to time I read, purposelessly and at random, encyclopaedias.

109

"It shouldn't be, 'She graduated from U.C.L.A.' It should be, 'She was graduated from U.C.L.A.'"

Pedantry.

110

Although I have enormous respect for Nero, I still don't quite get it about "contact" as a verb,

    or about vinegar.

111

I really do commiserate with my translator.

112

Greece: why does wealth so often breed inanity?

113

I'm beginning to come more and more round to the purist view of aesthetics.

The reason: Greek music.

Music which doesn't seem to have much connection with anything other than itself. (Even more so than color, which involves a certain inescapable association and synaesthesia.)

Even the lyrics, although not entirely irrelevant, are almost deductible.

And the music would remain the wonder that it is.

114

I want the **music**! Not all the fatuous blabbering **talk**.

115

Did it happen? Was it Enlightenment?

Twelve noon, March 2, 2001, at Epavli Gardens in Rhodos under, not a bo tree, but a tropical palm.

116

Brigitte Bardot: I'd like to shove some of her beloveds' dog shit right up her empathetic ass.

117

I think of dogs the way I think about flies, roaches, and mosquitoes.

118

Greeks have as hefty blinders and blinkers, although perhaps of a different sort, as anyone else.

119

I **still** think Greeks are the second worst drivers in the world.

120

All my life I've been trying to get a group of discoursing friends together, but with pitifully poor success.

121

I agree with Benchley:

There's a conspiracy amongst minim inanimate objects. When they fall, for example, they make a point of falling and bouncing and rolling to the farthest recess and least accessible nook.

And then there's this—that, out of the blue, they will occasionally pull their little disappearing acts.

122

DOMINIONS

The most powerful	sex
The deepest	memory
The sweetest	love
The most enslaving	food
The most stimulating	literature

(continued)

122-A

The most electrifying	drunkenness
The most wondrous	maps
The most entrancing	beauty
The most delightsome	travel
The most enigmatic	time
The most significant	goodness

123

Sometimes something magical occurs when one language is translated into another.

124

If I had to be reincarnated backwards, I would opt for Ibn Batūta.

125

The best saints are wrought from the worst sinners.

126

First impressions are usually the correct ones.

127

I'm getting to the point where I **murderously** dislike DJ's.

(Especially the ones who keep breezily turning the volume knob up and down as they interject their chatty bilge right in the middle of a song.)

128

I'm beginning to identify with Japan's Yukio Mishima.

Now, if only I had the courage.

129

There's no doubt about it: wildflowers are the most beautiful things on earth.

130

If I should die tomorrow, I still won't have missed:

early visits to Greece (**elafrá elliniká tragoúthia**)
hairline handball wins
extraordinary meals
intellectual insights/breakthroughs
Proustian wraiths

(continued)

130-A

extreme sexual excitements
idolized authors
early memories
literary excellences
great drunkennesses
overwhelming loves
picaresque travels
Magnum Opus laborings
exquisite massages
science-fiction reveries
nighttime staticky polyglot short-wave broadcasts
whispery philosophical musings.

131

DISAPPEARANCES

Angie Pappas	Chicago, Illinois
Ray Mammarella	Jacksonville, Florida
Wayne Hamm	Jacksonville, Florida
Anna Kyriakidis	Sao Paulo, Brazil
Ianni Christodoulou	Ano Kalamaki, Athens

(continued)

131-A

Chris Ignatiou	Kearny, New Jersey
Grigorios and Cleopatra Lioudakis	Rethimnon, Crete
John Grammaticas	Makriyialos, Crete
Gustavo Godoy	Jacksonville, Florida
	Havana, Cuba
Ray Pelstring	Cincinnati, Ohio
Ray Obert	Cincinnati, Ohio
Paul Georgiou	Limassol, Cyprus

(continued)

131-B

Mike Christou	Hampton, Virginia
Bill Lee	Jacksonville, Florida
Mihalis Lapatsis	Korydalos, Pireaus
Pauline Soubas	Charlottesville, Virginia
Jimmy Jacobs	Los Angeles, California
Norm Doomar	Jacksonville, Florida
Ed White	Jacksonville, Florida

(continued)

131-C

Zoi Gordon	Norfolk, Virginia
Tom Dummer	Sussex, England
"Tripoli" Pezzotti	Marone, Brescia, Italy
Ruth Leuenberger	Zurich, Switzerland
Etō Jun	Tokyo, Japan
Chris Critzos	Houston, Texas
Freddie Munsch	New York, New York

132

Actors-turned-writers; actors-turned-politicians/statesmen: such is the harlequinade we've come to.

133

Just about everyone betrays his childhood.

134

Who's to say that all the youthful enthusiasms, fervors, and certainties weren't the correct ones?

135

That T.S. Eliotian awareness of the uniqueness and never-for-all-eternity-to-return sublimity of each precious and wistful moment—is absolutely staggering and **CRUSHING.**

136

Shades of St. Augustine!

Another especial bench in Rhodos.

137

    I wonder if any notables and luminaries ever think about spastics, hunchbacks, midgets, wheelchair-captives, amputees, arthritics, asthmatics.

138

People who litter: I'd like to break their fucking face.

139

    A day without **payload**—whether it be sensual, aesthetic, intellectual, spiritual, whatever—is a day disemboweled and murdered.

140

There's no way of telling in advance, or even in the very happening, which moments will become **sub specie aeterni** moments.

(Like Wolfe's remembrance of "the fly...swallowed on the peach...and the mole on Grover's neck, and the Lackawanna freight-car, number 16356, on a siding near Gulfport.")

141

I saw my colleague and friend, Ray Mammarella, waste away and die from pancreatic cancer.

Nothing will ever make up for this.

142

For certain droning sonorous historical, architectural, cultural guides:

How is it that one can be intelligent, well-informed, mentally agile, linguistically adept, quickly aware—

and still be a nitwit?

143

People who don't mean what they say: so so many.

144

Brevity is not always the soul of wit.

145

Greek patriotism is about as bad as the American variety.

146

More holidays in Greece than you can shake another stick at.

147

My idolatry and adoration for Verne and Wolfe go far further than just sympathy with their views, admiration for their prowess, respect and acclaim and astoundment at their achievements;

they have to do with the very breath and rhythm of their cadences, the stamp and savor of their sentences, the pith and blood and purity of their every wisp and utterance;

they speak to the very core and innards and throbbing pulse of my being.

148

There's a certain special sadness that descends when one is let down by a friend.

149

I can't drive for ten minutes in Greece—not **ten minutes**—without getting either irritated, aggravated, or **EXPLOSIONAL.**

150

Sto kaló has to be the most beautiful expression on earth.

151

There has to be a God, so that the truth will be registered.

152

Love seeks perfection; sex can do with, indeed sometimes thrives on, imperfection.

153

It has taken me untold years to arrive at the very no-holes-barred limits of sex; which is where I should have been all along.

154

History buffs are like music buffs.

Both a little addlebrained and off.

155

Alex Comfort was quite right to analogize sex and gastronomy.

156

How flat and monochromed to be a monoglot.

157

I keep finding fault with Greeks, but then I'll come across some American Gothic "pitchfork" tourists,

and I will thank my lucky stars.

158

It was nice in Rhodes in winter.

Now comes the garbage.

159

If you drink enough **retsína**, all things are acceptable.

160

I always thought the English were one of the few peoples that aren't pushy.

The other day, along comes a group to shatter my illusion.

161

I don't like to struggle with my food.

162

Death is the Great Arbiter, the Great Unraveler, the Great Leveler.

163

Cyprus may be a backwater, but it's **my** backwater.

164

I can no longer deal with English prudery; I'd rather masturbate.

CYPRIOT EATS
(On a scale of 1-10)

rési	1
trahaná	2
pniyoúri	2
flaoúnes	2
eliópita	5

(continued)

165-A

shámishi	7
sheftaliá	7
haloúmi (salted)	7
haloúmi (unsalted)	8
haloúmi (fried)	9
loukánika	10
well-executed **loukoumáthes**	10

166

Stavrovouni Monastery, Cyprus

A world without television, radio, or **mirrors**.

It boggles the mind.

167

Sex and monasteries: oh how well they together go!

168

It occurred to me the other day that even being the planetary dictator would be just another job—albeit an interesting one—and somewhat of a chore.

169

Walking uphill is not exactly what I like to do.

170

How can one ever again take an Indian accent seriously, after Peter Sellers' zany and convulsive performance in **The Party**?

171

Some people will invariably sound affected, even if they aren't and don't mean to be.

172

So many smart and talented and knowledgeable and expert people all around.

And yet, in some fundamental way, stunted and retarded.

173

Evangelos Venizelos: the William F. Buckley, Jr. of Greece.

(Without the wit.)

174

It's hard to believe, but it can actually happen:

Innocent men who languish in prison for years and years.

Innocent men who languish in prison for years and years, and then are executed.

This is a terrible terrible terrible thing.

175

As I get older,

I more and more prefer to be with just me,

than with even the most interesting coterie,

or even, yes even, thee.

176

Politics, money-making, record-breaking, art, sport, study, research—all these pursuits that so absorb so many,

hold not a candle to sex.

177

(In essence, the language theme once again):

All other nationalities seem **simplistic** in the face of Greece.

178

I have to add **Pretty Woman** to my movie list.

179

In a truly civilized society, most red lights and stop signs would become "Yields."

180

"Closure" (as in "Those who suffered terribly from this terrible ordeal desperately need closure") is a terrible word.

"Utitz, Emil, 1883— (**The American Peoples Encyclopedia**, published by Grolier Incorporated, 1948-1963), German aesthetician and philosopher..."

I wonder what he was like, and about all the details of his life.

182

"Văcărescu, (**The American Peoples Encyclopedia**, published by Grolier Incorporated, 1948-1963), a Rumanian family... [the] niece, Elena Văcărescu (1868-1947), wrote verse and prose in both Rumanian and French. Her **Rumanian Ballads** (1905) was awarded the Favre Prize by the French Academy."

I wonder what she was like, and about all the details of her life.

183

The big mystery to me is how a good and spirited but otherwise unremarkable country like Greece can produce such remarkable and astonishing music.

184

I think I dislike Trent Lott even more than I did John Connally.

185

Trent Lott or Phil Gramm: now **that** would be an agonizing choice.

186

How mortifying it must be for French to lose its hegemony and world-wide sway to uncouth and upstart English.

Now isn't that just too too fuckin' bad!

187

Under-my-breath "Merde!" and "Fuck you!" are now becoming part of my core vocabulary.

188

Nothing, but nothing, is more false than astrology.

Even voodoo is less false.

189

Greek radio: every hour on the hour and on the half-hour, there'll be five or six minutes of unadulterated garbage.

The rest of the time, one might hear some truly beautiful music.

190

Radio philosophers are even worse than barber-shop ones.

191

I guess I would have to anoint Trent Lott.

At least, Phil Gramm isn't slimy-oily.

192

An excellent way to take in the wonder of **STRUCTURES** is to have a preferred seat on a city bus.

193

Little bitchy die-hards: pistachios that refuse to open up.

194

If you can't bear all the inanities on the radio, why don't you get yourself a CD and listen to your music uninterrupted?

Because on the radio there are surprises.

195

...with apologies for the last, definitely the last, time:

That TV butterfly, Fotini Georganta, is one sexy lady!

back home

196

I forgot, God I forgot! I forgot about all the lunacies and inanities, about the insipidity, the frigidity, the shallowness, the corniness, the religious looniness, the awful awful music, the unawareness, the rigidity, the angularity, the mindless exuberance, the overall tastelessness and vapidity.

But then, too, I did not really forget about the openness and friendliness and fairness and efficiency and decency

and overall goodness.

197

I've lost interest, my God I've lost interest! Lost interest in talk shows and the memoirs of Hollywood personalities and championship events and play-offs and World Cups and Super Bowls and lectures and exhibitions and fancy hotels and cruises and tourist destinations and Miss Universe pageants and Academy Awards and ceremonies and celebrations and holidays and elections and debates and speeches and prizes and a host of other things.

198

I don't ever want to talk to Larry King.

Not Live, not Canned, not Pickled.

August 15, 2002

Ex Cathedra

14th Encyclical

von Herrn Doktor Professor Peter Joannides

1

I don't think I've ever **resented** an American President as much as I now do George W. Bush.

2

A long time ago, my friend Cary was mightily enamored of Gene Tierney.

Something I could never understand.

Not that Gene Tierney was an unattractive woman. Quite the contrary.

But such an overwhelming ardor?

I'm sure Cary would probably feel the same way about my wanton obsession with Barbara Rush.

3

Sometimes one little thing can tip the balance, perhaps save a man from suicide, and be the entranceway to salvation:

a bowl of blueberries	a childhood memory
a wildflower	a snowflake
a butterfly	a leaf battered by heavy rain
The Children of Captain Grant	a noble deed
Thus Spake Zarathustra	a crystal
a little girl	a hummingbird

4

All along, I never could do anything partial.

5

Christian Arabs: what better combination could there be?

6

I never could understand what all the fuss was about: men having sex with men and women with women.

7

Every once in a while (even more than once in a while) the thought bubbles and surfaces:

U.S.A.: Looneyland.

8

The admittedly staggering and shiveringly awesome thoughts in Kant's ponderous **Critique of Pure Reason** could probably be quite adequately expressed in thirty well-written pages.

Or even less.

9

The yolk of an egg is the only part worth eating; the rest is poison.

10

Sometimes I don't think I know what I'm talking about.

11

          Gatlinburg, Tennessee has to be one of the ugliest places on earth.

12

          Every single thing (person, event) intimates some ultimate resolution.

But there has never been a resolution.

13

Gore Vidal never had a childhood; he was born an adult.

14

It's not the content; it's the manner.

15

Everyone is locked into the selfishness of himself, except for certain Catholic priests I've met.

16

Any movie with Robert Benchley in it, no matter what, is immediately sanctified.

17

It's amazing how much you can tell about a person in a very very short time.

18

I have such **ambivalence** for Garrison Keillor.

19

A **big** fish in a **big** pond: nothing less.

20

Sex at its most unbridled and intense is to the rest of life what Mr. Hyde is to Dr. Jekyll.

21

The Three Stooges

It just wouldn't ever work for me:

Curly could never take the place of Shemp.

22

The only **real** Charlie Chan is, of course, Sidney Toler.

Warner Oland was, however (adult perspective), the better one.

23

A definite no-no and barbarism:

Eggs in a garden salad.

24

That smug and self-congratulating noun "deal" is not to my liking.

25

If you live long enough, everything must be reinterpreted.

26

World Almanac

List of Deceased Actors

It's shocking to realize how little time some of them had.

27

If I were a trillionaire, I'd definitely have a harem.

28

One should live so as to **match** the wonders of childhood.

29

All these young people, with all of their E N T H U S I A S M S!

Just make me feel embarrassed.

30

If I had to be an expert on something, I would like it to have been, and to be: S E X.

On all the thinkabilities and extravagant possibilities; on all the **Kama Sutra** positions and threesomes foursomes combinations permutations and moresomes; on dildos and vibrators and aphrodisiacs philtres chains stimulants enhancers; on nymphomania flagellation fellatioism algolagnia satyromania; on every bodily part, every shade nicety detail nuance exactitude, every erotic fantasy fetish scenario playlet, every conceivable lustfulness reverie and shameless debauchery.

31

Who in this wide wide world, what blood-brother of my soul, would know and recognize the names of Bob Learce and Joe Bell?

32

Ayn Rand: a principled woman with some commendable ideas, but a little too intense for me.

33

I sometimes speak ill of the dead.

34

There is such a thing as instant dislike:

> Woody Allen
> Trent Lott
> John Travolta
> Dick Thornburg
> Bryant Gumbel

35

As there is instant like:

> Wallace Beery
> Tyrone Power
> Daniel Inouye
> Frank Reynolds
> Frank McGhee

36

So many things that happened, and were expected to recur and by-and-by recur...
                              happened only once.

37

I no longer have the time or inclination for digests, not even for digests of digests.

38

Suddenly,
              all my old friends have become terribly precious to me.

39

Wretched and horrific as the deeds of Sept. 11 are, that inescapable American cant just can't help but settle in.

40

Of all the obsessions and fetishes in this world, the Proustian one is the best.

41

Every few days I learn new words, new facts, new perspectives; new awarenesses swim into view; old ones become modified or outmoded; an ever-wondrous and ever startling thrust into new territory, new and indistinct mazes and dimensions.

It is as if I have always been, and continue to be, in a sort of fog, that "O lost," "lost" lostness of Wolfe.

This far more the human condition than any "encyclopaedic stance" of all the hubristic, strutting, self-plumed, pitifully fraudulent commentators and dispensers of Olympian Wisdom: William F. Buckley, Jr., Stephen Jay Gould, George Will, Milton Friedman, Robert J. Samuelson, Lance Morrow, Charles Krauthammer, Roger Rosenblatt, et al.

42

Here I am, trapped.

And my mother raised me to do great things.

43

I am definitely left-handed.

I write, throw, serve, forehand, punch, block, fence, fork, shave, wave—with my left.

And yet I bowl, pitch softball, scissor, arm-wrestle, pull the trigger, kick a football, manipulate a mouse, pull up on a lawnmower, throw the dice—with my right.

What physiological mysteries lie therein!

44

Maybe part of what is wrong with this world is that people obey orders.

45

The greatest science-fiction movie ever made:

Invasion of the Body Snatchers

46

There is something sad about landlocked countries.

Except for Bolivia.

47

Surely Phileas Fogg (Chapter XXX: In Which Phileas Fogg Simply Does His Duty) has to be one of the highest types of men.

48

Arabs are the most truly hospitable people in the world, more so than even Greeks, Italians, Turks, East Indians, or anyone else.

49-A

There is such a thing as the truth.

We may never be able to discover the truth, but it is there nonetheless.

For example, the exact number of pennies in Smith's trouser pocket at 10:30 A.M. on March 19, 1974 (the day that Smith visited the Smithsonian in Washington).

So, too, in the moral and aesthetic sphere.

Who is truly the bravest, who is truly the most honorable, truly the most honest, truly the most good and compassionate?

What is truly the most significant and worthy creation?

49-B

The truth may be a far cry from the historical record.

We may never know.

But the realization that there is this truth is a great comfort.

We say, "Only God will ever know."

And this is the closest to a meaningful concept of God.

50

Spare me, please, from Greek intellectuals who patronize Americans.

51

Wouldn't it be ironic if, in the end, I turn out to be an Arch-Conservative.

52

Wittgenstein was undoubtedly a genius, but I can do without all the mannerisms and theatricalities (and, quite possibly, incivilities).

53

I don't love people who love dogs.

54

Tony Blair is a babbler.

55

Tell me, who reads and who cares about the philosophy of Alfred North Whitehead these days?

56

In **entry 55**, one can easily substitute for "Alfred North Whitehead" any of the following:

        C.D. Broad   F.C.S. Northrop
        Benedetto Croce   John Wisdom
        J.M.E. McTaggart   Ralph Barton Perry
        Hermann Lotze   Herbert Feigl
        Hans Vaihinger   C.I. Lewis
                Alexius Meinong

And a host of others.

57

After first and foremost, sex, and second and secondmost, food, I wouldn't mind being an expert on color.

58

Holidays, flag days, commemorations—after hours notwithstanding—nothing and **NO PLACE** should ever be **CLOSED**.

But should be manned by generously numerous shifts, 24 hours a day, 365 days a year.

59

Americans can be intelligent, healthy, decent, witty, sensitive, aware, but they lack a certain something—difficult to lay hold of—that practically every other nationality has.

60

Oprah Winfrey: deeply shallow.

61

For all my years, I thought of cream cheese as some sort of poor relation to all its more illustrious kin—brie, camembert, roquefort, kasseri, feta, etc.

Now I have come to realize (and have decided) that it can hold its own with, indeed get the best of, any and all of them.

62

What if... what if... every quip, every intimate conversation, every expletive, outburst, complaint, gossip, saccharine theatricality, sexual whispering, self-muttering in a car—were somehow to be recorded and stored (by some ultra-technological aliens)?

and be capable of being played back in all its detail and clarity.

63

How fortunate!

To have been born into the premier language of the planet.

64

99.5% of all jobs are awful, and 99.5% of all job-holders are slaves.

65

One senses immediately that Hanan Ashrawi is an interesting woman.

66

Courtly and polite white Southern gentlemen are really decrepit.

67

After I eat, I am dead to the world and worthless for, at the very least, 45 minutes.

68

Love Affair ('39)　　**An Affair to Remember** ('57)
Irene Dunne, Charles Boyer　　Deborah Kerr, Cary Grant

Sorry, but this time the re-make is better than the original.

69

Like some before me,
　　　　　　　　I answer only to God.

70

I've always had a secret envy and grudging admiration for entrepreneurs.

I am not one.

I am more of a reflective, ruminating, mulling, enjoying sponge.

71

Among other things I will do when I win the lottery is to have constructed a personal shower, sort of like a waterfall, with enormous volume and pressure.

To be followed by a **WHOLE** towel-studded, blow dry **ROOM**, with enormous jets of hot dry air blasting from everywhichever direction.

72

Fascinating and delightful it would be to visit some of these remote islands: Clipperton (France), San Benedicto (Mexico), Isla Blanquilla (Venezuela), Isla Alejandro Selkirk (Chile), Sala y Gòmez (Chile), Christmas Island (Australia), Île Amsterdam (France), Bouvet (Norway), Heard (Australia), Balleny (New Zealand), Johnston (U.S.), Peter I (Norway), Macquarie (Australia), Borden (Canada), Aleksandra Ostrova (Russia).

73

What hurts today, may not hurt tomorrow.

74

And, needless to say: what doesn't, may.

75

I have no interest in speaking to the World.

Just to a few friends.

76

My **Ex Cathedras** speak volumes.

77

Patriotism is pretty far down the totem pole of my fealties.

78

I can make a whole meal out of the **skins**, and nothing but the skins, of several fried chickens.

79

I have respect and deference for researchers, craftsmen, and engineers.

80

One of my past lines that I'm rather proud of:

"Acting is a despicable profession."

81

No surgery is ever easy.

82

I simply can't settle for anything less than winning the lottery.

83

Thomas Wolfe is the greatest ever American writer. In fact, one of the greatest writers of all time and place.

There is no doubt about this.

84

Philosophers are adolescents.

85

The music of Trinidad has to be one of the most cleansing in the world.

86

I forgot to add (Professor) Cornel West to my list of instant dislikes.

87

Bill Cosby: a kind of low-level awareness, and so a kind of low-level hubris.

And thus not too reprehensible.

88

Dirty talk is great talk.

89

As put off and even repelled as I was by Malcolm Forbes, I really did like his epitaph.

90

A truly honest person would admit that plastic has it all over glass.

91

Old Age Homes, Nursing Homes, Assisted Livings, etc.: Thousands upon thousands of dregs and discards all squeezed together and living out their appointed days, listening to the tickings and tocks of monotoned clocks, staring into the vacancies of space, waiting waiting, some shouting obscenities, others in catatonic poses, herded into mess halls, wheeled into recreation rooms, marking time in the hallways...

It is enough to make you want to blow your brains out.

92

At least 5.999 billion souls on this planet have no idea what real **QUIET** is,

    nor of the pleasures it affords.

93

It may not have been a blockbuster film, but it means a lot to me:

They Drive By Night, with George Raft, Humphrey Bogart, Ann Sheridan, Ida Lupino, Alan Hale, and George Tobias.

94

I have such **ambivalence** for Hugh Hefner.

95

The blind, the deaf, the maimed, the tortured, the hungry, the uprooted, the trapped, the diseased, the chronically pained, the malformed, the disfigured, the retarded, the brutalized, the lonely...

It is enough to make you want to blow your brains out.

96

I can do without the politics and attitudes of James Kilpatrick and William Safire, but I do like people who love language.

97

Many problems would be solved if it really sunk in that we don't live forever.

98

I am inordinately sensitive to unpleasant accents. Half my tirades and vitriols, and even more than half, are probably attributable to this.

99

Hegel and Bradley were right.

(In a poetic way, of course.)

100

There is something surreal—ludicrous—impertinent—obscene—topsy-turvy—downright ugly about Pat Buchanan quoting T.S. Eliot.

101

There is nothing more sullied and graceless than the half-baked.

102

I couldn't give a two-penny fart who I alienate.

103

Benny Hill has brought me a lot of pleasure over the years.

104

Rum (scotch, bourbon, gin, vodka) at night; Dubonnet under the sun.

105

I want nothing less than to be **DICTATOR** of **THE PLANET**.

106

Epicurus may very well be the greatest of philosophers.

107

God is neither wise nor compassionate nor benevolent.

He created dogs.

108

In the end, it is a Japanese meal that is the most ambrosial and spiritual.

109

I never quite realized it before, but Douglas MacArthur really was a horse's ass.

110

So many, so many misplaced loyalties.

111

People in EDUCATION have to be the most flabby, mishmashed, gobbledygooky, and unaesthetic of thinkers.

112

I'm convinced there are some good Mexicans.

113

March, 2002

I saw that Miss again on that early morning television exercise show.

Her name is Page Langton.

She is gorgeous, ravishing, luscious, gorgeous.

I could easily lose my head and everything else over her.

114

It's their **voices** that undo American women.

115

Mercifully, not all American women have hard, metallic voices.

116

The advertisement in the Personals of "The (London) Times" placed by Ernest Shackleton in 1914 when he was recruiting for his Antarctic Expedition:

"MEN WANTED

for hazardous journey, small wages, bitter cold, long months of complete darkness, constant danger, safe return doubtful, honor and recognition in case of success."

Around 5,000 applicants answered the call.

I haven't read anything so beautiful for a long, long time.

117

Gays are generally more sophisticated than straights.

118

One can have great, even colossal, virtues and still be strictured, even pathetic, in so many other ways.

119

Always, always, especially when Nature imperiously calls, the Women's Rest Room is discovered first.

120

That line of T.S. Eliot that keeps running continually through my brain:

"In a minute there is time
For decisions and revisions which a minute will reverse."

121-A

And some others:

"To spit out all the butt-ends of my days and ways?"

"Of lonely men in shirt-sleeves, leaning out of windows?"

"The moment in the arbour where the rain beat,"

"Quick, said the bird, find them, find them,"

121-B

"Quick now, here, now, always—"

"But all the way, in a dark wood, in a bramble,
On the edge of a grimpen, where is no secure foothold,
And menaced by monsters, fancy lights,"

"I said to my soul, be still, and wait without hope
For hope would be hope for the wrong thing; wait without love
For love would be love of the wrong thing...
So the darkness shall be the light, and the stillness the dancing."

"Till human voices wake us, and we drown."

122

All the nasty things I said about the French notwithstanding, I genuinely would welcome my **real** French counterpart.

123

I call the traffic light at Ivey and Southside "The Shit Light."

124

When hacks quote Thomas Wolfe, it turns my stomach.

125

For me to enjoy sex, I have to have a story.

126

There's no hubris quite as foul as Southern hubris.

(Ernest Hollings, for example.)

127

"There are no free lunches."

What a silly and untrue thing to say. Lottery winners and inheritors get free lunches every day.

128

Every once in a while, William F. Buckley, Jr. is lucid.

129

It's one thing to have a traffic light where one is needed. It's quite another to have a "Shit Light" like the one at Ivey and Southside.

130

In spite of T.S. Eliot's "every moment is a new and shocking Valuation of all we have been," there are certain inviolable constants in my life: the early New York years, Jules Verne, Thomas Wolfe, F. Nietzsche, Logan Pearsall Smith, Nona, the semi-desert, the rain forest, filet mignon, handobōru, H.G. Wells, first contact, rum 'n coke, Greek music, sunlight, sauna, erotomania, hydrophilia, the wonder of a new trip to uncharted and untrodden places.

131

I love little lizards.

132

I don't forget slights.

133

The Dave Scales 12th Annual Handball Tournament
Jacksonville, Florida
April 19-21, 2002

It has finally dawned on me that I can't move like I used to.

134

When actors depict actual historical personalities, it's time to vomit.

135

"A wake-up call."

Another of those bromidic, groupie expressions, along with "where he's coming from," "the bottom line," and "sends a message."

136

I am the only one who knows all about myself.

137

I wish I had noted the names and addresses of all those certain good and decent working people I have run across over the years—waitresses, bus boys, ticket agents, short-order cooks, flight attendants, pilots, mechanics, secretaries, plumbers, librarians, cashiers, firemen, policemen, nurses—conscientious, quick, sharply efficient, dependable, knowledgeable, honorable, responsible—each of whom I recognized immediately as special and sterling—so that, in the event I become the planetary dictator, I can put them in positions of trust and authority, and have them work for me.

138

Two types of sick people:

Those who swim scores and scores of uninterrupted laps in a pool, up and back, up and back, without stopping.

Those who have millions and millions of dollars at hand and still want to be mayors of large cities.

139

Sex blots out everything else.

140

So many doctors are such fraudulent assholes.

141

I don't know why so many look down their nose at the Waffle House.

Unjustifiably so.

142

One day, in Tennessee (in Knoxville, no less!), it was like being in Ambato or Cochabamba.

(It was the 14th of May, 2002.)

143

I don't like to stay at Indian-owned-and-run motels, not because of any untoward judgment or prejudice...

(in fact, the very reverse has long been true—decidedly and happily pro-Indian)

but because of the literal **smells**.

144

Dal has to be the nastiest culinary concoction ever devised by the nose of man.

145

Stephen Jay Gould is dead.
Am I supposed to feel badly?
For all the snotty things I've said?
Well, the fact is I do feel badly.
Although I can't really take anything back.
Nor, in truth, do I really want to.
Nor do I think I ought to.

146

A forgotten snotty remark:

Stephen Jay Gould: an intellectual Bryant Gumbel.

147

We live in a wonderland, and don't even realize it.

148

He who likes his bacon half-burnt and his calamari tentacles charred is a man of good taste.

149

He who likes his steaks well-done and his bacon uncrisp is a man of poor taste.

150

Please, **ANY** music other than American music!

(We're not talking here of Glenn Miller, Tommy Dorsey, Cole Porter, etc. and the old days.)

151

I don't know which low-class is more low-class than the other: low-class Americans or low-class Greeks.

152

I simply do not have the patience to bring a woman off if she requires a master mechanic.

153

No one, in the whole history of show business, was more suited to his part than Carroll O'Connor/ Archie Bunker.

154

I'm beginning to thoroughly dislike ads.

ALL ads.

Including the cute and clever and amusing and imaginative ones.

155

The perfect scrambled eggs: flecks of white in a furrowed sea of yellow; jiggly-soft and moist.

156

Thomas Wolfe is my Shakespeare.

157

Nothing **terrifies** me in quite the way a headache does.

158

"Buckingham Palace hosts a rap session, with all sorts of chic 'artists' and entertainers, including the remaining Beatles."

All in the swirling vulgarities together: Queens, Presidents, Screaming Longhair Guitarists, University Presidents, Archbishops, Leather Boys, Nobel Laureates, Senators, Heavy Metalists, Governors, Mayors.

159

What a mockery and travesty are celebrity writers! I want people to say, in the same breath, "Salinger, Pynchon, and Joannides."

160

Many people know how to work; very few, how to play.

in Greece

161

The curse of the modern world: unwanted music.

162

What a wonderful world it would be: one without flies, gnats, ticks, mosquitoes, sharks, jellyfish, roaches, and dogs.

163

I just can't help it: I stand in awe of automobile mechanics.

164

May all mufflerless motorcyclists/motorscooterists fry in the furthermost fires of hell.

165

Greeks: the greatest time-murderers the world has ever known.

166

All it takes is **one** fly.

167

Sometimes I think Oblomov had the right idea.

168

To think of everything all together all at once: an impossibility.

And yet the very highest of possibilities.

169

Nothing can cement a relationship quite like shared food and drink.

170

When I'm away from home, I really do enjoy reading the **International Herald Tribune**.

171

That fucking bench in Rhodos is **MY** bench, and I wish all the Greek and tourist retards would keep their butts off.

172

Greece: It still amazes me—how such a rough, insensitive, braggart, noise-polluting, often louty people can produce such delightful music.

173

I sometimes have a daydream: that in some distant future all of Rhodos will have just a handful of human enclaves, utterly quiet and utterly clean and ultra-technological, sharing the island with the desert sagebrush and thyme and lizards and wildflowers and little fishes, and that all the vulgarities will have been left far behind, all the discos, come-ons, gauderies, fast foods, fancy lights, with just a few ruins of these now to have become a bygone era superimposed upon that even further bygone era.

174

It's easy to skewer people you don't personally know. Much harder to do so with those you do.

175

Fuck all organization men.

176

What makes restaurateurs think that, aside from a bowl of soup (or variations thereof), a fork **AND** knife isn't required for anything else one might order to eat.

177

If only those who hear one speak in a fractured second language only knew what wit, humor, incisiveness, creativity that same one may be capable of in his own language.

178

I've yet to have a blind date work out.

179

Greek radio: How I hate every hour on the hour, the witching hour when the music stops and the shit starts.

180

Sunday is not the day to do anything in Greece except stay at home.

181

Never have I experienced such a contrast of utter serenity so very close to a bustling city center as I have that of Epavli Gardens to the screeching madness and mayhem of Mandraki (Rhodos)—**literally**, a six-minute walk apart.

182

Michael Crichton: **Airframe**.

The last sentence in the following paragraph is without doubt the best sentence in the book:

> Jennifer hated to wake up with some guy in the room. She hated everything about it, the sounds they made breathing, the smell coming off their skin, their greasy hair on the pillow. Even the catches, the celebrities who made her heart skip over candlelight, looked like soggy beached whales the next day.

183

Why do some drinking glasses sweat and others don't?

184

Nothing more icky than to struggle into a shirt while sweaty.

185

Food and sex are very much alike.

186

I don't know which is worse: a woman with a tattoo or a woman with a dog.

187

There's a lot of bullshit on TV in Greece.

188

There are also some excellent documentaries on TV in Greece.

189

You haven't lived Megisti unless you've climbed those steps.

190

Flat-chested girls often have great legs.

191

Spindly-legged girls often have great busts.

192

All my life I've used the services of fancy hotels without being their paying guest.

193

The ultra-technological and the effortlessly simple,

merge.

194

If it weren't for Lotto, I probably would have long since killed myself.

195

Unless the company is very special, I'd rather have my gin and tonic by myself.

196

The secret to creative solitary drinking is, once started, not to have to **move**.

197

If I hear the word "**maláka!**" one more time, I think I'll scream.

Oh what wit and originality! what savoir-faire! the little clubby cliquey gangy rib-poking cachinnating Greek teddy boys.

198

You don't realize what garbage American music is until you come to Greece.

(Again, we're not talking about the old days.)

199

I've had it with the young.

200

I find the Business News to be an utter bore.

201

After all the heat and the glare, there come the nighttime summer breezes bathing the Greek islands: how to render, what superlatives can one possibly use?

202

Greek DJ's, Stateside DJ's, DJ's from around the world: oh how they all love the chatty chummy ring of their own voices!

203

B. Tatakis. For many years a professor of philosophy at the University of Thessaloniki.

A good and kind and decent man.

204

    Some people in Greece work hard. Thanklessly, tirelessly, hours-upon-hours-and-days-upon-days-and-no-letup hard.

205

My esteem for Jules Verne borders on the holy.

back home

206

    The older I get, the more I suspect that consciousness has but scant connection with what is, and with what is really going on.

April 1, 2004

Ex Cathedra

15th Encyclical

von Herrn Doktor Professor Peter Joannides

1

Body language in a swimming pool is even more revealing.

2

An indefatigable sex machine along with a caring human partner for before, (and even during), and especially after: the ultimate sexual scenario for a woman.

3

It always amuses me when people say, "He can speak nine languages fluently." There is no way in hell one can speak nine languages fluently unless he has also lived nine lives fluently.

The absolute upper limit is five.

4

　　Stoplights are prejudiced against me. They take malevolent delight in turning red just as I approach. If one were to calculate the percentages, far more have I been the victim of red than the beneficiary of green.

　　The laws of probability have been violated. There is evil intent out there.

5

　　Here I am, a geographical man trapped in an electronic age.

6

　　Ofttimes, it is those in ivory towers who move the world.

7

　　I like making the first drink for assembled company.

　　I definitely want someone else to make the second. (For me, too.)

8

The only thing that can't be duplicated is what is new.

9

I'm beginning to think Oregon is a good state.

10

Everybody sings for his supper except inheritors and lotto winners.

11

Some of these generalizations I make are a bit asinine.

12

Hendrik Hertzberg is a little bit snotty, but he writes well and has some good ideas.

13

The thought of **specializing** in something—anything—more or less repels.

14

All my eggs in one basket: that's the way it is with me.

15

Everyone is locked into his language.

16

I'm not sure all those so-called great men were really so great.

17

I like my History straight.

18

Fujiyama at a distance is one thing. Fujiyama close up is like the sebaceous skin horrors that Gulliver encountered with the Brobdingnagians.

19

There is something sad about landlocked countries.

Except for Bolivia.

(And maybe Switzerland.)

20

How I love the word (and the thought): Heist!

21

Spokesmen for the President and the State Department are a slimy breed.

22

Slimy positions make for slimy breeds.

23

The dead are so so dead.

24

One of the highlights of my life is to read the **Britannica Yearbook** every Fall.

25

No writing, not even the very best of writing, has ever even remotely approached capturing the Fullness of experience.

26

Sex: Power without Profundity.

27

Conversation among professional philosophers sounds more and more like twaddle every day.

28

The mountains of North Carolina in summer: the Whole Outside is air-conditioned!

29

If I had to be an expert on something, and we've already mentioned sex and food and color, then let it be wildflowers.

And after that let it be liquor and liquor bottles.

30

I swoon when I enter an ample and well-stocked liquor store, with its plethora of phials and decanters and flagons and carafes, of all shapes and sizes and labels and colors, all arrayed and wondrously displayed, and know of the promise of the myriad treasures, all encorked and embottled within.

31

In spite of his intelligence, imagination, virtuosity, I don't think I would like Salman Rushdie.

32

Thomas Wolfe: Here we have a great writer—one of the greatest writers of World literature—worried about a little mousy asshole like Bernard DeVoto.

33

Some old Cypriots I have known view Death in such a sweet and natural and accepting and unfrantic way,

That I can only stand in awe and respect and wish I were they.

34

The death of so many friends and loved ones has pierced the joy of winning the lottery.

35

I don't have to give reasons for not liking someone.

36

Driving down U.S. 19, from Port Richey to Dunedin, Florida, in a certain frame of mind, and with a certain way of looking at things (the myriad structures), can be downright exhilarating.

37

There is such a thing as creative masturbation.

38

Oriana Fallaci: Whatever else may be wrong with her, she has spirit.

39

The fact that I don't particularly want to be the planetary dictator anymore,

Is precisely the reason I should be.

40

The opening pages of Wittgenstein's **Philosophical Investigations**, in which he compares words and tools, language and games, are some of the most beautiful passages of all literature.

41

I am tempted to say that all forms of consciousness are equally valid.

42

Nothing but nothing beats traveling.

Not touristing.

Traveling.

43

I hate it when trees, clouds, telephone poles, latticeworks, buildings, gargoyles, canopies obstruct and blot out the sun.

44

Given the more or less traditional delineations of sexual perversity, it is amazing what a huge percentage of the population is sexually perverse.

45

Ken Burns' documentary on New York was preeminent and superb.

I don't know if his others can ever match such a standard of excellence.

46

Writers who go on the lecture circuit are such self-congratulating, prancing, cockish clowns.

47

What I want is a lot of money with absolutely no strings attached.

48

No politician (statesman, if you will), no matter how enlightened and well-meaning, can escape slime and moral turpitude.
It is the nature of the beast.

A Dictator, however, can.

49

If we have to have a politician, it might as well be John Kerry.

50

If one can afford it, why one would take an interest in anything other than food, sex, travel, literature, friendship, beauty, and sports—is beyond me.

51

I'm no vegetarian!

52

With the possible exception of J.D. Salinger, there is no living writer that I have greater respect for than Andy Rooney.

53

To not be famous and to be rich (but not known to be rich) is the best way to be.

54

One of these days I'm going to **STOP** reading, learning, traveling, socializing, inquiring, exploring, sniffing... and try to digest and make sense of all that hitherto has gone on.

55

The worst sight under God: severe chronic pain.

56

My ideas and opinions of thirty years ago: about the same, but not all.

57

Things that are considered common knowledge, I learned about just the other day.

58

I can tell if a woman enjoys sex just by looking at her.

59

Caipirinhas: after the 2nd you are at the pinnacle of awareness and well-being; after the 3rd you enter another Universe, hardly commensurate and hardly rememberable.

60

I don't care what scientists, specialists, researchers, experts say—

I insist and **know** that drafts have something to do with colds.

61

I really write for my alter ego.

But in order to reach him, I must go through all the garbage of publishing, publicity, reviews, interviews, critiques, catalogs, best-seller lists, what have you.

62

I can't give up. I owe it to all the purities that have graced my life.

63

I want to run this planet.

If I can't do that, I just want to have a good time.

64

I love to go to flea markets and revel in their multiplicities.

65

The one thing that endeared me to Mustapha Kemal was his admiration for H.G. Wells.

66

Pete Hamill seems like a likeable guy.

67

We seem to be at the mercy of accidents, illnesses, spouses, offspring, scams, friends, neighbors, family, employers, criminals, political upheavals, wars, economic downturns and fluctuations, natural catastrophes...

Maybe Epictetus was right.

68

I've always disliked saccharine adults who patronize children.

69

I bet not **all** children liked Mister Rogers.

70

Isn't it strange how a kindness once done is so fondly remembered after so many years:

Howard Fast taking the trouble to personally answer a letter sent as a lark by a teen-aged boy back in the late forties.

71

It's better to be a bird than a pig.

72

There are **lots** of good Americans.

73

Spanish-speaking radio announcers always **sound** sleazy to me, even though they may, in fact, not be so.

Portuguese-speaking ones never do, even though they may be so.

74

In many ways, I'm just a pussycat.

75

Strange how a film seen long ago becomes more and more worthy with the passage of time.

When I first saw **The Incredible Shrinking Man,** I would have given it a B-.

Ten years later it became a B+.

A few more years, and it got an A-.

It is now a straight A.

(Who knows, in another ten years, it may even warrant an A+.)

76

The same things could more or less be said about **An Affair To Remember**.

77

I really would like to get to know Pete Hamill.

78

All these macro-events that I absolutely can do nothing about!

79

The hoi polloi can no more understand great literature than the animals of a forest could grasp the dit-dots of a Morse Code transmission.

80

There is one thing that can definitely be said for Norman Mailer: he admires the right people.

81

What a hyper-polysyllabic language Greek is!

82

Time has a way of making friends out of acquaintances.

83

Everything fluctuates, but my love for Italy has ever remained the same.

84

Corn bread: hot and buttered and freshly-made and finely-textured and **at its best**: something silken and supernal.

85

There's something I like about men who stick with the same woman for their whole life.

86

Of all my mentors, the one most dear to me was Prof. Armistead Gordon at the University of Virginia, if only for having introduced me to the quiet and unassuming treasures of Lafcadio Hearn and **Kamongo** and **Trivia**.

87

I resent not being able to do exactly what I want to do, whenever I want to do it.

88

I never really did understand what Marshall McLuhan was talking about, then.

I do now.

89

Crowds, audiences, groups, assemblies, lectures, committees, conventions, conferences make me sick.

90

George Will: I always knew he was a jerk.

91

What adult achievements, exploits, pinnacles, prancings can ever hope to match the wonder of a child.

92

Nietzsche said, "Keep holy thy highest hope."

Without meaning to sound disrespectful, my highest hope is to win the lottery.

93

So many doctors are such artful frauds.

94

The Miss Universe contest: All that variegated and wondrous pussy out there!

95

Gentle as I really am, yet with unperturbability could I torture the torturers.

96

Not winning the lottery is like being a cripple.

97

I don't want to hear **Aesop's Fables** in English.

98

Although his accent leaves a lot to be desired, Senator Dodd of Connecticut would probably make a good lama.

But, just as with Ralph Nader, it wouldn't do for him to be the High Lama.

99

In order to fix the world, I have to run the world.

100

I don't think **The Catcher in the Rye** is near as good as **Franny and Zooey** or **Raise High the Roof Beam, Carpenters**.

101

All those literary twerps who tried to bring J.D. Salinger down.

102

John Updike on J.D. Salinger

As much as I like and respect Updike, he should not, I think, patronize his betters.

103

I guess I haven't lived such a bad life:

Not counting airport terminals, and taking into consideration that nations have here and there changed their names and boundaries, I have managed to set foot in slightly more than half the countries of this world.

104

It may not seem like such a big thing, but getting cosmopolitan Costa Achillopulo to visit me in Jacksonville, Florida was a definite coup and by no means an insignificant feat.

105

Most everyone is beholden to language—molded and structured and subservient to it.

A very few take hold of it, surmount it, and forge new compositions and perspectives with it.

106

There is absolutely nothing wrong with any kind of sex.

(But perhaps this ought not to be too loudly proclaimed, as it might take the fun out of it.)

107

Everything that ever happened—every detail, nuance, nicety—is recorded and stored in the mind of God.

108

There's no more inane conversation than that of shallow New Yorkers.

109

John Updike: a very high-class groupie.

110

It's been a long, long time since I've come up for air.

111

So many voices, so many moods, slants, tempers, sways, all vying and jostling to suck me in.

But in the end I refuse to be sucked in.

112

I wonder if Warren Buffett knows about orchids and their intimate and symbiotic tie to insects? I wonder if Warren Buffett knows about astronomy, philosophy, evolution, history, etymology, the myriad linkages of multiplex structures? I wonder if Warren Buffett knows about travel, not corporate travel, but open-ended on-the-road travel, about winging it and the having of new adventures and living the picaresque existence? I wonder if Warren Buffett knows about lust, not just sex, but overwhelming, overpowering, decadent lust? I wonder if Warren Buffett knows about literary pantheons, about Marcel Proust, about succumbing and throwing caution to the winds, about psychoanalysis, aesthetics, immolation, altered states, about passion, wonder, and eccentricity?

Warren Buffett does know about money.

113

Eulogies are becoming boring, burletta, and banal.

114

I'm not really very quick. Or witty.

And I hate to argue.

115

The thought often crosses my mind: I could easily have been born a dwarf.

116

There are more locker-room philosophers in the U.S.A. than in the rest of the world combined.

117

Those department-store knick-knacks and bric-a-brac that abound for the mentally retarded—porcelain turkeys, ceramic elephants, platitudinous murals, fake jewelries, maudlin homilies and gushy words of love and wisdom couched in flower-dappled special booklets, speckled iridescent glasses, bromidic statues, replicas and cherubs—suffocate me and make me sick.

118

As I get older, I find myself starting to reappraise the reappraisals.

119

America: the land of clones.

120

In my heart of hearts, I want to be only with people like Lord and Lady Glenarvan, Paganel, Thalcave, Major MacNabb, Captain Mangles and Mary Grant, Wilson and Mulready, Tom Austin the mate, Olbinett the steward, and the good sailors of the "Duncan."

121

Somewhere in the misty ambages and tendrils of the songs of Carlos Gardel, one of my souls is lost and crying.

122

There is something pathetic about older men trying so hard to be young ones.

123

The best bathroom shower I've ever encountered was at a relatively modest hotel in Sofia, Bulgaria near the city bus station—a veritable torrent of cascading wondrous water.

The second best was at the Rice Planter's Inn in Walterboro, South Carolina.

124

A real accomplishment would be to somehow wangle an indulgence from the Indian authorities to visit and be escorted to the Nicobar Islands, be protected from the sandflies, mosquitoes, and indigenous tribes, be catered to and made superbly comfortable, and get to snorkel in the limpid opalescent waters.

125

I have such ambivalence for Bill Maher.

(Bill Maher is not such a bad guy. But why does he want to dispense his wisdom to crowds?)

126

I don't like to work at what I eat. I don't want to peel, pick at, tease out, tweeze out, shuck, shell, pare, snip, separate, or ferret out.

I want what I eat to be ready, and uncomplicated.

127

John Updike: He knows everything. He's read everything. He's up on everything. He's privy to everything. He writes about everything. Philosophy, biography, literary criticism, American mores, the vernacular, minor Hungarian poets, Sanskrit derivations. And not only that, but finds the time to write novels, short stories, and his own poetry as well.

He is truly THE ENCYCLOPAEDIC MAN.

The intellectual **par excellence**.

128

It's not the ideas of Republicans that offend me. (For all I know, they may be right about many things.)

It's their psyche.

129

Here I am with a third grade education in Greek and a Ph.D. grade in English.

130

I'm no great lover of apples, pears, or grapes.

131

Somehow the idea of female announcers with British accents on American radio doesn't sit well with me.

132

Memory can play tricks.

133

Wolfe's rendering of a rushing, galloping train:

click, clack, clackety-clack...click, clack, clackety-clack...hip, hop, hackety-hack... stip, step, rackety-rack...putrem...putrem... putrem quadrupedante quadrupedante quadrupedante putrem putrem as with sonitu quatit ungula campum quadrupedante putrem

The greatest onomatopoeia of all literature!

134

If only we could get rid of the music and the patrons at the Waffle House.

135

I suspect they will say of my work:

The greatest concentration of contradictions in the history of literature.

136

O'Reilly and Woody Allen:

I simply **CANNOT BEAR** watching them. Not even for five seconds.

137

The law of gravity can, at times, infuriate me.

138

Even in Hawaii, Iowa Americans stick out like sore thumbs.

139

I always thought of Hawaii as somehow **ahead** of everyplace else.

There is a sense, though, in which it's still a backwater.

140

It is one thing to cut corners.

It is quite another to cut corners with friends.

141

I give my friends the benefit of every doubt. But there comes a point...

And when that point is reached, the whole edifice crumbles.

142

Corollary to #1

It just fascinates me: how much I can tell about a person from the way he swims in a swimming pool.

143

Mexican-American cuisine is better than Mexican cuisine; Chinese-American is better than Chinese; Indian-American is better than Indian.

144

Time stretches and retracts.

It s t r e t c h e s and s t r e t c h e s at the beginning, and retracts at the end.

145

Some people are so dirty—or so sick—that you don't even want to have dirty sex with them.

146

A lesson learned a bit late: You can get used to practically anything.

147

The trouble with Viagra is that you have to make love on an empty stomach.

148

A **PHYSICAL** disorder: the only legitimate reason for suicide.

149

"Don't eat red meat. Don't eat shellfish. Avoid salt. Avoid sugar. No alcohol should be imbibed. Don't smoke. Keep out of the sun."

FUCK YOU!

150

The most cheerful country in the world: **B R A Z I L**.

151

Sometimes I have nothing but contempt for just about everything in this world, except goodness and kindness.

152

I was always taught that whenever you have items in a series set off by commas, it is optional whether to include the final comma between the penultimate and the final item (joined by "and").

I don't know why, but it mightily disturbs me if that final comma is not put in.

153

I can probably put away 50 scallops at one sitting.

154

Long ago,

I read what I read when I read it.

I don't have the time or inclination to read any longer.

155

I think I could listen to the best of Greek music for all eternity.

156

The last warm feelings I had for the French was back in 1949 with Edith Piaf and **La vie en rose**.

157

Bill Frist, Senate Majority Leader (2003), is totally alien to me.

158

I don't like prolific writers.

159

I once tried to E X P L A I N **Zarathustra**.

It was a disaster.

160

I can smell that something is an ad from a million miles away.

161

The third best bathroom shower I've ever encountered was at the Dream Inn in Daytona Beach, Florida.

162

I don't like smart-ass remarks about the writers I love.

163

I'm not sure the cartoon world is any the less real than the real world.

164

Arabic music and song drive many I know right up the wall.

Personally, I like Arabic music and song.

165

All professors have a certain stink about them.

Some more, some less, but always that unmistakable stink.

166

I say again:

A good brie restoreth my faith in the Universe.

167

Sometimes I love curly frizzly leafy salads so much—

I think I'm a rabbit.

168

God?

Why not simply another name for the truth.

Which we may not ever know.

And which perhaps we cannot ever know.

169

There's nothing wrong with unmanicured lawns.

170

Women shouldn't broadcast football games.

171

The closest thing to religion, for me, is Jules Verne.

172

"A Brief Encounter"

Isn't it this way? With practically everyone? With practically everything?

173

Oh how I'd love to diddle all those early-morning young-lady newscasters, all freshly-bathed and perfumed and groomed and just brimming with curvature and sexual vigor and bloom.

174

Oh how I love good pornography!

175

There's nothing wrong with American Jewry, except for that cloying self-consciousness.

176

Good sex always needs a story line.

177

No matter how good an individual production might be, Drama (Theater, Movies) is an intrinsically inferior art form.

The lowest of the fine arts.

178

Films that depict actual historical personalities are mostly garbage.

179

Buddhism is probably the best religion (certainly the most sophisticated).

But all religions are more or less silly.

180

When you love somebody, it doesn't matter if they're even a monster.

181

I'm for Fred Hoyle.

Even if The Big Bang is true, it is still subservient to, and subsumable under, The Steady State.

182

Nothing bores me more and so utterly than football philosophers.

183

I must really be getting mellow in my old age:

The other day the thought crossed my mind that possibly, just possibly, there might be something to be said for Opera.

184

The thought of anyone with a Southern accent having any sort of jurisdiction over me is both revolting and umbrageous.

But perhaps I shouldn't make such sweeping generalizations. After all, there was Jimmy Carter.

185

Some more jokers I can't bear watching for not even five seconds:

Chris Rock, Dennis Miller.

186

Paramecia can't help doing what they do; centipedes can't help doing what they do; hamsters can't help doing what they do. And neither can pelicans, caribou, bull frogs, billy goats, polar bears, crabs, snails, tigers, and mandrills.

It's pretty obvious that monkey-men just as much can't help doing what they do.

187

When I say "Portuguese," I mean "**Brazil!**"

188

I never dreamed I'd ever hear myself saying this:

Sometimes I think sex is such an overpowering taskmaster, such a demanding, disrupting, upsetting, expensive, time-consuming, unappeasable pursuit, such a monkey on my back, such a nuisance—that maybe I'd be better off without it.

189

If there's one thing I don't want to do in life, it's to take care of a dog.

190

It really does amuse me: how sometimes a third-rate Greek will patronize me because I don't speak the language as well as he does.

191

I like sandals.

I don't like shoes.

192

The language of educational theory: the most unmitigated mishmashed gobbledygooky sonorous-sounding quackish turgid pretentious crap that can be imagined.

193

Why do I have such difficulty with the genitive in Greek!?

194

It's too bad that such a stunning woman like Catherine Zeta-Jones should have an American voice.

She should have remained a European—with a European voice.

195

I wonder sometimes whether I am not really as stupid as I seem to be when it comes to certain matters.

(Such as curriculum committee deliberations, economic predictions and fluctuations, Supreme Court briefs and dissents, Dow Jones-Nasdaq, Capital Gains, computer viruses, educational criteria and Affirmative Action, Presidential caucuses and primaries.)

Maybe it's just that these things simply don't interest me.

196

I greatly admire those who planned and executed the Hong Kong Airport, with all of its attendant bridges, tunnels, and thruways.

197

To see and hear one on television tells me infinitely more about him than do any of his writings.

Example: Noam Chomsky

198

Patients on stretchers waiting to be transported in the corridors of a hospital remind me of airplanes waiting in line on the tarmac of a major airport.

199

There is such a thing as British louts.

Something I wouldn't have thought possible 40 years ago.

200

What's the difference between cricket and baseball?

www.ingramcontent.com/pod-product-compliance
Lightning Source LLC
Chambersburg PA
CBHW071259110426
42743CB00042B/1100